Contents

Acknowledgments

Even critics favourable to Werner Herzog – and not all of those who have
written about him have been that – tend to write off his *Nosferatu*, tellingly
subtitled 'Phantom of the Night' in its German and French versions, as a
minor work, an inferior remake of Murnau's great original. Murnau's
classic film and the seminal novel by Bram Stoker on which it was based
have also had their detractors, from the important historian of the horror
movie, Carlos Clarens, to André Gide, who have denigrated the former,
and the many critics and editors who have detected 'shoddy writing' in the
latter. I admire all three, though in the present short study Stoker and
Murnau can figure only as forebears of Herzog. So far from being a mere
remake, Herzog's film seems to me a remarkable work in its own right,
entitled to an honoured place among important films produced in the
German Federal Republic during the 1960s and 70s – the period that
produced what has become known as the 'New
German Cinema'. Into that cinema, dominated by Alexander Kluge,
Rainer Werner Fassbinder, Wim Wenders, Volker Schlöndorff,
H.-J. Syberberg and J.-M. Straub, Herzog introduced a note wholly
personal to himself yet no less significant for the spirit of its time than the
work of these other directors. The later chapters of the present book will
try to make this particular note audible.

I have, as always, benefited greatly from help of various kinds given
me by friends and colleagues, including Hans-Michael Bock, Werner
Hüllen and Roger Pearson – and from the careful scrutiny of Rob White,
the editor of the BFI Modern Classics series. Some peripheral books are
cited in the Notes, but the Select Bibliography lists only those works that
have helped me come to terms with my main subject. I hope that this
sparse listing will be taken as an expression of my gratitude to their
authors. For the opinions consciously put forward, and the errors
unconsciously incurred, I am alone responsible.

1 From Dracula to Nosferatu

Like Mary Shelley's *Frankenstein* and Stevenson's *The Strange Case of Dr Jekyll and Mr Hyde*, Stoker's late Victorian novel belongs to a cherished class of nineteenth-century fictions in which 'an unusual individual in touch with private fears at a time when these fears were shared by the outside world consciously or unconsciously exploited the link between the two'.[1] *Dracula,* never out of print since its first publication, is also a filter through which folk beliefs, rural and urban myths, and historically conditioned as well as perennial psychological experiences, have passed into the ken of successive generations. Much of this is sexual: vampirism, as Stoker presents it, involves sadistic and masochistic practices, symbolic rapes of men, women and children, sudden changes from virgin to whore, and violations of jealously protected inner and outer spaces by vampire-hunters; neither the bodies of men and women, nor bedrooms, tombs, asylums, chapels, are sacrosanct.[2]

Social implications involve aristocratic violations of bourgeois proprieties, disastrous incursions of eastern strangers into western cities, capitalists 'sucking blood' – a metaphoric usage that Stoker's contemporary Karl Marx made peculiarly his own.[3] Freudians could detect instances of 'the return of the repressed', ancient fears returning to life – the dead coming back to plague the living, revenants and ghouls, succubi and succubae, lamias, empusas and striges – while Jungians could have a field-day searching for denizens of the collective unconscious where Shadow battled Anima. Medical fears also found an echo in such works: vampiric incursions could recall outbreaks of bubonic plague, smallpox, venereal disease (Stoker himself, like many of his contemporaries, may have suffered from syphilis), cholera, influenza and, more recently, SARS and AIDS. *Dracula* enshrines a version of the *Doppelgänger*, the spectral double beloved of German writers and film-makers: the vampiric Count may be seen as Jonathan Harker's double, acting out repressed desires that come to the surface when Jonathan is confronted by three vampire women (one of whom seems strangely familiar!) before Dracula chases them back with his homoerotic 'This man is mine!' And vampirism, as we meet it in Stoker's novel, is spilt religion: it parodies the Eucharist and needs a panoply of crucifixes and communion wafers (along with garlic and pointed stakes) for its defeat.

Dracula derives his name from a historic figure: Vlad Dracula, a fifteenth-century ruler of Wallachia, named after the Order of the Dragon into which his father had been received – though 'Dracul' (dragon) also meant 'Devil' in Romanian, an appropriate sobriquet in view of his legendary cruelty that involved impaling hundreds of victims at a time. Many of his brutal deeds took place in neighbouring Transylvania, famous for the exploits of Countess Elisabet Bathory, who sought to rejuvenate herself by bathing in the blood of freshly killed young girls – just as Stoker's Dracula grows younger as he sates himself on the blood of his male and female victims.[4]

Stoker spent six years studying vampire lore, in the British Museum and in other libraries, through conversations with Arminius Vambery, a Hungarian professor of Oriental Languages whom he met and befriended in London in 1890, and through extensive acquaintance with many vampire-plays performed in London (often translated from French Grand Guignol), penny-dreadfuls like *Varney the Vampyre, or, The Feast of Blood*, travel writings and a rich Romantic tradition that was very much alive in Victorian England. There were poems by Goethe, Coleridge, Byron, Southey and Keats, featuring vampiric beings of both sexes, 'Gothic' novels by Anne Radcliffe, 'Monk' Lewis and Charles Maturin, and one story in particular, penned by Stoker's fellow-Irishman Sheridan Le Fanu, 'Carmilla', which had taken its place in a remarkable collection of Le Fanu's short stories entitled *In a Glass Darkly* (1872). The influence of Le Fanu's tale is most clearly visible in the chapter from *Dracula* which Stoker later excised and which was published separately as 'Dracula's Guest'. The most powerful influence of all, however, was the work of Wilkie Collins, especially *The Woman in White* of 1860, whose multi-narrator and multi-document structure *Dracula* mirrors, and whose plot includes a wicked foreign nobleman and scenes in a Victorian lunatic asylum. The appearance, in *Dracula*, of a ghostly 'Lady in Black' is a nod to Collins as surely as a child's invocation of a 'Bloofer lady' echoes the 'boofer lady' of Dickens's *Our Mutual Friend*.

Stoker's novel has perennial appeal; but it is firmly rooted in Victorian soil. It shows a bourgeois businessman travelling into foreign regions in quest of improved sales and in a spirit of enterprise. An English aristocrat, a wealthy American and a spirited woman who is more than a swooning invalid or her complement, the 'Angel in the House', all join him in the task of foiling a foreign danger that is threatening the stability of Victorian marriage and Victorian society. In this task of thwarting an invader from eastern lands they are helped by a scientist and occultist from a friendly western power, the Netherlands. The setting is London, which had, by the 1890s, become the biggest city in the world; battening on its teeming life, Dracula becomes an ancestor of more recent power-hungry figures like Blofeld or Goldfinger or the controllers of SMERSH.

Stoker firmly sketches in a background of scientific discovery and technological innovation; information is imparted, collected and stored not only in handwritten diaries but also in documents produced on typewriters and speech recorded on phonographs. Van Helsing, the Dutch vampire-hunter, is a disciple of Jean-Martin Charcot and adopts his guru's theories of hysteria along with his experimental practice of hypnotism. In fact, Van Helsing and other male characters are themselves subject to hysterical attacks, proving that one need not have a womb (*hustera*) to be so afflicted. There is much talk of medical theories, their limitations and the gradual crossing of frontiers that formerly guarded unknown territories of body and mind, as well as the application of recent medical practices like blood transfusion.[5]

Above all, *Dracula* enshrines in its two principal female figures, Mina and Lucy, two conceptions of women that complemented one another towards the end of the nineteenth century. On the one hand there is fear of the disruptive effects female sexuality might have within a patriarchal society: Lucy, who begins as a girlishly gushing, well-brought-up young lady, has 'polyandrist' fantasies when she is courted by three eligible young men at the same time; under the vampire's bite, she turns into a polymorphously perverse sexual predator and paedophile who has to be hunted down as mercilessly as the foreign Count who changed her from Victorian virgin to voluptuous devourer of blood. 'The blood is the life', quotes the mad Renfield from Deuteronomy 12:23, tempting us post-Freudians to equate blood and semen.

Mina, on the other hand, is the male vampire-hunters' invaluable helpmeet: she is more steady and intelligent than any of the British and American males, and by keeping and assembling all the relevant records, she becomes the putative author of the novel in which she is a character. One of her principal weapons is that typewriter which transformed the career prospects of so many women at the end of the century; and though, like Lucy, she is bitten by the vampire, her help enables the male hunters with their fearful panoply of phallic weapons, ranging from scalpel to stake, to track the attacker to his lair and, by defeating him, restore Mina to her admirable self. The only one of the fearless vampire-hunters who dies is the American; and after Van Helsing, his task completed, has returned to the Netherlands, three happy English couples are left to raise their families. As Martin Tropp has commented:

All the distortions of the maternal role, the gruesome tastes of Dracula's women, Lucy's nocturnal activities, Mina's nursing of grown men, and even Dracula's opening a vein in his chest and forcing Mina to drink his blood – are answered by the birth of Mina's child. Mina becomes a wife and mother who is useful, competent and independent ... Though they set out to save her, at the end of the book it is Mina who leads the reluctant band of men into the twentieth century.[6]

Stoker's *Dracula* completed a process begun, in England, by the Byronic Lord Ruthven of John Polidori's *The Vampyre*, written in 1816 but first published in 1819: the transformation of the evil-smelling revenant of peasant folklore, come from the grave to torment his fellow-villagers until they staked him or cut off his head, into the aristocratic being who could travel to distant parts (provided he carried with him some of his native earth) to work his mischief. He remained a shape-shifter, assuming the garb and manners of the sophisticated society he invaded as easily as changing into a bat or some other beast – though he could be recognised for what he was by his failure to cast a shadow or appear as a reflection in a mirror. The novel of which he is the central character has been subject to the most varied interpretations, many of which have been summarised in Maud Ellmann's admirable edition:

Dracula has been interpreted as a figure for perversion, menstruation, venereal disease, female sexuality, male homosexuality, feudal aristocracy, monopoly capitalism, the proletariat, the Jew, the primal father, the Antichrist, and the typewriter. But Dracula is all these things, and more: he stands for the return of the repressed, the contents of which are forever shifting. For this reason he can never be pinned down: he continues to change shape, beyond the covers of Bram Stoker's book, in the minds of his insatiable interpreters.[7]

Among these interpreters and reinventors, film-makers of many nations have been prominent – none more so than one of the greatest German directors of silent films, F. W. Murnau (Friedrich Wilhelm Plumpe, 1888–1931). Murnau and his scriptwriter Henrik Galeen plucked out a term Stoker had found for the undead, 'Nosferatu', placed it in their title – *Nosferatu. Eine Symphonie des Grauens* – and had the chronicler who acted as narrator give it a resonance it has never since lost:

Nosferatu, does not this word sound in your ear like a call of the bird of death. Beware of uttering it, or the images of life will fade into shadows, spectral dreams will arise in your heart and feed on your blood …[8]

This cinematic 'symphony' of 1921–2, in its turn, inspired Werner Herzog to another set of variations, to be considered in Chapter 4, which were as significant for the Germany of the Western Republic that followed World War II as Murnau's had been for that which had its all-too-brief life after World War I. Both, however, drew freely on the late Victorian novel whose author uncovered, partly unconsciously, deep-seated desires and apprehensions, and had, in the process, transformed a peasant superstition into a potent modern myth.[9]

2 Tradition and Alienation

Between Murnau's *Nosferatu* and Herzog's film lies the most disgraceful period of German history: the murder, and complicity in murder, of millions of people born into the 'wrong' religion or race, with sexual orientations, mental handicaps or nomadic dispositions that made them 'unfit' to be part of the new order, or with political beliefs other than those officially decreed; and with robbery on an unprecedented scale whose beneficiaries, whether large or small, became accomplices with their own stake in the smooth working of the industrialised, bureaucratically administered and sadistically enforced policies of death. What this did to those who followed the generation that had spawned, supported or tolerated the criminal Nazi regime is vividly illustrated by one of thousands of separate anecdotes told and collected over many years. This one, from an interview with a thirty-two year-old Bavarian woman published in 1979, the year Herzog's *Nosferatu* appeared, is typical of many:

I first heard about things that the Nazis had done when I was eight. There was this little girl who came to school day after day weeping. I finally asked her what was the matter, and she said that her father had just been imprisoned as a war criminal. He had been accused of killing hundreds of inmates in a camp. I raced home and blurted to my father: 'Her father did this! Did you do it, too?' There was a terrible scene. My mother said to me: 'How dare you speak with such disrespect! I forbid you ever to bring up the subject again.' To this day, I have not had the courage to confront them a second time.'[10]

The guilt and evasions of the parents could poison the lives of the children.

Post-war German film-makers born too late for complicity had an analogous problem: many of their senior colleagues who had not been murdered or forced into emigration had been active at a time when their work served the efficient propaganda machine run by Josef Goebbels, their careers furthered by the disappearance of some of the finest talent of the Weimar Republic. Moreover, a great many of the films made in the first two decades *after* the end of the war were not to the taste of the most intelligent

and socially aware young men and women eager to make their own contribu-
tion to the renascent film industry of the Federal Republic. Some of their
criticism of 'Papa's Kino' was unfair; but fine works by Helmut Käutner,
Erich Engel, Peter Lorre and others were lost in a welter of self-pitying
'rubble films', 'Sissi'-type sentimentalisations of history, crudely formulaic
regional melodramas, filmed operettas, petty-bourgeois comedies, Edgar
Wallace adaptations and apologetic depictions of German officers and men
in World War II, untainted by, and usually resentful of, Nazi ideology.

The first open sign of revolt came in 1962, in the so-called
'Oberhausen Manifesto', which rejected post-war German film-making in
favour of new principles largely formulated by the chief ideologist of this
earliest manifestation of what came to be called the 'New German
Cinema', Alexander Kluge. Herzog was not one of the signatories of this
manifesto, and despite friendly relations with those who subsequently
made their mark in its wake – notably Kluge, Volker Schlöndorff and
Rainer Werner Fassbinder – remained aloof from the various groupings of
the Federal Republic as well as those of the German Democratic Republic,
which followed its own socialist path, with official controls a maverick like
Herzog could hardly have borne. No one, however, felt more strongly than
he that he was part of a 'fatherless generation': as a German, who felt that
his people, who had produced 'the greatest philosophers, composers,
writers and mathematicians', but had in the space of only ten years,
'created a barbarism more terrible than had ever been seen before'; as a
Bavarian, who loved the region into which he had been born but knew
that it had also been the very cradle of the Nazi movement; and as a man
who resented his own father, a feckless and largely absent figure.[11]

Though Herzog was born in Munich, in 1942, he spent most of his
childhood in a remote village in the Bavarian mountains, with no cinemas
to go to and no telephone, guided by a strong-minded divorced mother
who led Werner and his siblings into smuggling expeditions in nearby
Austria. His original name, Stipetić, points to Balkan ancestry, but by
changing his name to a German one, he asserted his loyalty to a Germany
whose immediate past he deplored but whose traditions he respected. He
welcomed the chaos that followed the collapse of the Nazi regime: 'It was

anarchy in the best sense of the word. There were no ruling fathers and no rules to follow. We had to invent everything from scratch.'[12]

As a teenager, however, Herzog saw his first films, and knew that this was the art to which he wanted to devote his life. Yet he soon saw that 'anarchy' and 'inventing everything from scratch' was not enough to express what he knew was in him. He was, ineluctably, not just German, but specifically Bavarian – in the spirit of that most imaginative (and disturbed) of kings, Ludwig II of Bavaria, builder of dream-castles and promoter of Wagnerian opera. Even in his remotest travels he remembered his Bavarian roots: the jungles of *Aguirre, der Zorn Gottes* (*Aguirre, Wrath of God*, 1972) were to him intensifications of Bavarian forests, and one of the most impressive passages of *Nosferatu* is filmed in a region of mountain, stream and wood in which he had wandered as a boy. He needed roots, and he needed legitimate traditions.

By making *Nosferatu* he took account of that need in four different ways. First, encouraged by the great historian of Weimar film, Lotte Eisner, he linked his work to what he believed to have been the *legitimate* tradition broken off in 1933 by producing a homage to, and variation of, the work of the Weimar film-maker he most admired, Friedrich Wilhelm Murnau. Second, he connected his very German film with wider European traditions by choosing, for leading parts, an actress who had honed her craft and made her name at the end of the French *nouvelle vague*, and a man whose graphic and literary work, produced mainly in France, had a well-deserved European reputation – Isabelle Adjani and Roland Topor. Third, he shot much of the film in the Czech Republic, using English as the lingua franca best understood by his international cast, and released it in three languages, though he always maintained that he thought the version in German the most authentic, despite some necessary dubbing.[13] Last, he chose in Florian Fricke a composer who accompanied his images with music that mingled singing voices with electronic instruments unknown before the war. Part of an experimental tradition the Nazis, with their philistine tastes in art, had excoriated as 'degenerate', this music had already shown itself capable of engaging young people through the concerts of the Popol Vuh group whose leading spirit was the classically trained Fricke. Herzog used the music of Richard Wagner too, to cleanse it of the cult the Nazis had made of it, although he recognised, as everyone must, that in one important respect Wagner's ideology had anticipated that of the Jew-baiters, whose murderous activities, however, that great composer could not have anticipated.

Nor was Herzog the only one of the talented generation that created the New German Cinema who sought to connect his work with older German traditions or traditions outside his native country: Volker Schlöndorff served his apprenticeship in France, Wim Wenders looked to the American cinema and Rainer Werner Fassbinder saw Douglas Sirk's work as an important model – as Detlev Sierck, the latter had made distinguished melodramas in German studios before leaving the uncongenial atmosphere of Nazi Germany for the United States. Herzog too learnt from the American cinema: Griffith, for him, was 'the Shakespeare of film-making'.[14]

Once he had left his Bavarian village and acquired a Gymnasium education that concluded with the Abitur in 1961, Herzog became an inveterate traveller, learning his excellent English in Manchester, where he worked for a few months, and as a Fulbright Exchange visitor at Duquesne University's film department. When his American visa expired, he went to Mexico, where he had experiences that fed into many of his films (including, as will be seen, *Nosferatu*). He made his first film, a short documentary about body-builders that demythologised heroic myth (*Herakles*, 1962), and formed his own film company, where he was soon joined by his brother, Lucki Stipetić, as principal production assistant and business manager. A film script he composed won a prize named after the most prominent producer of scripts in the silent era, Carl Mayer. This was turned into Herzog's first full-length feature film, *Lebenszeichen* (*Signs of Life*) in 1967, made on the Greek island of Kos, which inaugurated two practices he would maintain throughout his later career: first, making films outside Germany, some as far afield as the South American jungles, the Australian bushlands and troubled states in Africa and the Middle East, others nearer, like parts of *Nosferatu*, in Holland and Moravia; and second, composing, and usually publishing, a narrative version of the film he was about to make, which he regarded as a separate work on which the film would play medium-specific

variations. Many prizes followed, and many attacks, in a career that has so
far produced eleven full-length feature films and over thirty thematically
related documentaries. However, regardless of how much time he might
spend on location abroad, Herzog remained a consciously German film-
maker whose outlook was affected by German traditions and social and
intellectual developments in the Federal Republic.

At the age of fourteen Herzog became, briefly, a born-again Christian in
the arms of the Catholic Church that was so strong a force in the religious,
social and political life of his native Bavaria; but he was most affected by the
existentialist outlook that shaped much of German intellectual life after World
War II, with its notion of the individual seeking to assert his existence and
realise his essence in a world of *Gerede* (idle gossip) and *das man* (the
impersonal collective). 'Existential' is in fact a key word in many of Herzog's
autobiographical and explanatory utterances. As he travelled about the world,
he became ever more convinced that even after the defeat of Nazism 'our
civilisation is like a thin layer of ice upon a deep ocean of chaos and darkness';[15]
that civilisation may, in fact, destroy innocence, as it chews up the titular hero of
The Enigma of Kaspar Hauser (1974), whose German title indicts a world in
which everyone is out for himself and God has set Himself against all (*Jeder für
sich und Gott gegen alle*). No one has ever depicted hell on earth more
powerfully than Herzog in *Lektionen in Finsternis* (*Lessons in Darkness*, 1992)
which was shot in Kuwait after the Iraqi invaders had been driven out. His
images of what the retreating invaders had left behind reinforce the lesson
many of us have drawn from Dante's *Inferno*: what we imagine of hell is drawn
from what we know is going on in our own terrestrial world.

The alienated imagination that conceived this and other such films
found nourishment in the Federal Republic, when disillusion set in after the
'economic miracle' of the Adenauer era, when the doctrines of *soziale
Marktwirtschaft* that sought to combine the free working of market forces
with an element of social justice were countered by an 'extra-parliamentary
opposition' that began with a radical student movement and widened into a
more general assault on consumerism and bourgeois complacency. Many
different groups kept up the German tradition of missing the middle way:
radical Leftists who could, like the underground Red Army Faction, become

murderously violent; counter-culturists with ideas about sexual liberation and freeing the imagination through drugs; 'Green' ecologists who soon squabbled among themselves; and the large *Ohne mich* (Without Me) brigade, which devoted itself to private enrichment and satisfactions without social or party loyalties in the era of the Great Coalition between Christian Democrats and Social Democrats that began in 1966. By 1978, the year in which Herzog conceived *Nosferatu*, the Federal Republic had become 'a discouraged republic' (H. von Hentig), in which the voices of the prophets of doom were heard more and more loudly as terrorism, the oil crisis and worldwide signs of recession began to tarnish the remarkable recovery Germany had made after the destruction of 1945, and the socialist experiment of the German Democratic Republic had taken a turn that hardly offered a desirable alternative.

However disillusioned Herzog may have been with the world he encountered, and however often he observed failure in the weak, like Kaspar Hauser and the three German outsiders who travel to Wisconsin in search of a better life (*Stroszek*, 1977), or in the strong, like Aguirre, he never entirely despaired of the possibilities of the human spirit that manifested itself in dreamers and artists like the central figure of *Die grosse Ekstase des Bildschnitzers Steiner* (*The Great Ecstasy of Woodcarver Steiner*, 1975) or in people who overcame terrible handicaps, like Fini Straubinger, the blind and deaf heroine of another of his great documentaries, *Land des Schweigens und der Dunkelheit* (*Land of Silence and Darkness*, 1971). Nor did he overlook the possibility that even if the enterprise on which you set out ended, as most enterprises do in his work, in failure – the failure of strong rebels and predestined victims alike – there was a chance of salvaging something, some existential satisfaction, as the hero of *Fitzcarraldo* (1982) manages to do within the Herzogian empire of darkness that appears so starkly in his *Nosferatu*. He has also shown, notably in *Gott und die Beladenen* (*God and the Burdened*, 1999), in the impressive film he made with the composer John Taverner, *Pilgrimage* (2001), and in his reverential documentary about Tibetan Buddhism, *Rad der Zeit* (*Wheel of Time*, 2003), the power of ritual and religious devotion to inspire those who had not lost, or had rediscovered, their faith. In

Pilgrimage such faith is conveyed in music as well as in images of pilgrims and penitents in South America and Russia; and from the worn record that plays an aria from *The Magic Flute* in *Kaspar Hauser* onwards, music plays an important part in Herzog's films, not least because he saw an analogy between his own filmic art and that of a composer as well as a conductor of musical works. This shows itself not only in his frequent collaboration with Florian Fricke but also in his use of ethnic chants and the music of composers like Gesualdo, Vivaldi, Couperin or Wagner on his soundtracks, either to reinforce or to counter the tenor of his images.

Paul Cronin, in his introduction to the collection of his interviews with the film-maker in *Herzog on Herzog*, has declared that his interviewee's work 'is not in the tradition of the German romanticists'.[16] It depends, I suppose, on what one means by 'in the tradition of', but that there are affinities between Herzog's work and German Romanticism would be hard to deny. His very first feature film, *Signs of Life*, updates a short story by Achim von Arnim, one of the key figures of that movement, who here exhibited an interest in extreme states of the human psyche that he shares with Herzog. Romantic too is Herzog's admiration of the work of Caspar David Friedrich, which has influenced the disposition of figures and the lighting of many of his films – including *Nosferatu*. Even his admiration and use of Wagner indirectly looks back to Romanticism, for the composer found musical equivalents for the many Romantic themes and motifs, from veneration of past German glories in *Die Meistersinger* and revivals of Germanic myth in *Der Ring des Nibelungen* to the love-in-death motif of *Tristan und Isolde*, that pervade his operas. Equally Romantic is Herzog's interest in the 'Nightside of Nature', a phrase the Victorians adapted from Gotthilf Heinrich Schubert's *Ansichten von der Nachtseite der Naturwissenschaften* (*Scrutinies of the Nightside of the Natural Sciences*, 1808) and which describes very well the atmosphere that permeates German Romantic tales of terror, from Tieck to Hoffmann. To overlook this strand is to miss something important in his work: his ability to assimilate such influences while still producing films that unmistakably bear his signature.

His relation to German Expressionism shows a similar pattern. Like the dramatists and film-makers who are seen as part of that movement, Herzog is adept at projecting moods and inner dispositions outwardly into the world; like them he sees the father–son conflict as a sign of society in crisis; like them he uses the complicated technology that produced the cinema for projections into a pre-technological world or attacks on the spirit that worshipped science, technology and rationalism while distorting the benefits they brought – yet here too he remains his own man, even when paying tribute to Murnau and seeking to attach the New German Cinema to a 'legitimate' tradition broken off by the advent of Nazism.

Assimilation and variation also characterise the relation of Herzog's films to earlier genres, even before *Nosferatu* made this process more visible than it had previously been. *Kaspar Hauser* is a kind of dysfunctional *Heimatfilm*,[17] revealing how a beautiful provincial environment and regional bourgeois value systems may destroy innocence instead of nourishing and sustaining it. *The Great Ecstasy of Woodcarver Steiner* rehabilitates the mountain film, the *Bergfilm* that had become a vehicle of masculine heroics and (like the *Heimatfilm*) of blood and soil ideology, as it portrayed lone individuals pitting themselves against nature and their own passions, or using their mountaineering skills to defend their beloved region against foreign enemies. Woodcarver Steiner's ski-jumping, with its elegant flights, represents a conquest of gravity – of the pull of an earth that produces the materials out of which Steiner fashions his works of art, an art that follows in the footsteps of great medieval and fifteenth-century woodcarvers like Tilman Riemenschneider.

Aguirre is a Herzogian counter to the *Abenteuerfilm* that had served, in Nazi films like *Carl Peters* of 1941, to extol colonialising adventures in foreign parts. Aguirre, who regards himself as 'the wrath of God', is a more powerful and driven figure than Hans Albers's incarnation of the German adventurer, Peters, but Herzog shows the vanity of his ambitions by leaving him, at the end of his film, helplessly circling in the midst of a stream, on a raft invaded by monkeys, while silent forests concealing unseen enemies loom threateningly on the banks. The regions he has invaded can no more be a 'home' for Aguirre than the beautiful landscapes and cosy village interiors of *Kaspar Hauser* could be for the foundling hero of that seminal work.

Herzog has also emulated, in his own fashion, the many directors who have adapted classical works of the German stage for the screen:

Murnau's *Faust* (1926), Friedrich Zelnick's *Die Weber* (*The Weavers*, 1927, after a play by Gerhart Hauptmann), Gustav Ucicky's *Der zerbrochene Krug* (*The Broken Pitcher*, 1937, a play by Heinrich von Kleist) are famous examples. Herzog's favourite dramatist is Georg Büchner, as may be seen from the quotations or near-quotations built into *Kaspar Hauser*, and it is Büchner's *Wozzeck* that he fashioned into a vehicle for Klaus Kinski after completing *Nosferatu*. *Nosferatu* itself, of course, is a deliberate exercise in the 'vampire film', that sub-genre of the horror film that has flourished uninterruptedly in world cinemas ever since Tod Browning's *Dracula* followed John Balderston's stage adaptation and showed how Stoker's aristocratic protagonist could become a figure of cinematic legend. Herzog had not seen Browning's version when he made *Nosferatu*; but he had seen Roman Polanski's *Dance of the Vampires* (1967) and used a variant of its ending to great effect when giving a Herzogian twist to the plot pattern established by Murnau.

In 2001 Herzog tried to convey his sense of the Weimar Republic and the rise of the Nazi Party in a feature film entitled *Invincible*. It centres on two Berlin celebrities of the day, the Jewish strong man Zizhe Breitbart and the clairvoyant Hanussen; and while it contains some fine fantasy sequences it is, in my opinion, a deeply flawed work. Its central conception of Hanussen as a crypto-Jew from the fringes of the old Austro-Hungarian Empire, who made speeches celebrating Hitler as the potential saviour of Germany in order to assure himself a post as Minister for the Occult in a future Nazi government, is as historically unlikely as the presentation of Himmler, in 1932, as a drunken womaniser who sips wine from an elegant woman's shoe. The film fails as surely as Ingmar Bergman's *The Serpent's Egg* (1977), and for similar reasons; but great directors are not infallible, and everyone is entitled to the occasional experiment that does not come off. Such failures do not devalue the achievement of a director and writer who fashioned original films – films that could not be mistaken for the work of any other – out of his strong sense of tradition and equally strong feeling for the alienation and anomie he sensed among his contemporaries and compatriots.

3 Teamwork

Though Herzog had good relations with other directors who contributed to the flourishing New German Cinema of the 1960s and 70s, and closely collaborated with one of them, Herbert Achternbusch, on *Herz aus Glas* (*Heart of Glass*, 1976, another, specifically Bavarian, Herzogian take on the *Heimatfilm*), he was very much his own man and went his own filmic ways. He did not, for instance, join Kluge, Schlöndorff, Fassbinder and Edgar Reitz in their collective exploration of Germany in the shadow of terrorism and retaliatory violence, made in 1977–8 and entitled *Deutschland im Herbst* (*Germany in Autumn*). Most of his films were made under the auspices of, and released by, his own production company, founded in the mid-1960s. For *Nosferatu*, however, simultaneously released in Germany as *Nosferatu – Phantom der Nacht* and in France as *Nosferatu, fantôme de la nuit*, Herzog's outfit was joined by the German TV channel ZDF and the French Gaumont Company, and cut a distribution deal with 20th Century-Fox. While taking account of this international dimension by casting two French and two German actors in principal parts, and following his usual practice of selecting for minor parts suitable types recruited locally, including many who were not professional actors, his team consisted of what had become, by 1979, something of a Werner Herzog repertory company.

The most important members of that team, for *Nosferatu*, were the actor Klaus Kinski and the principal cinematographer, Jörg Schmidt-Reitwein. Schmidt-Reitwein had experienced what he himself described as his 'baptism of fire' when shooting Herzog's documentary *Fata Morgana* (1970) in the summer heat of the Sahara (who but Herzog or Erich von Stroheim would have thought of filming in such conditions?) and then enduring imprisonment in Cameroon when, as so often happened to Herzog and his team, they became embroiled, innocently on this occasion, in altercations with the local inhabitants. They were in fact mistaken for mercenaries engaged by one side or the other, in the wars of the Congo, Nigeria and Chad.

In the case of *Nosferatu* the quarrels with the inhabitants of the Dutch city of Delft, which stood in for the German Wismar in Herzog's film, centred on his importation of hundreds of Hungarian rats, originally white but painstakingly dyed grey and blow-dried to save them from pneumonia, which the Dutch thought a danger to their city, whose canals already had a rat problem. Schmidt-Reitwein had been on far more hazardous expeditions: on one occasion climbing to the edge of the crater of a volcano predicted to erupt within days. From all of them he had brought back images of landscapes and people that matched his director's vision and led one critic, Franz Schöler, to describe him in 1971 as 'one of the greatest cameramen of the last twenty years'.[18] Herzog, who often wielded a hand-held camera himself, thought him ideal for *Nosferatu,* because he had

a good feeling for darkness, threatening shadows and gloom, in part because just after the wall went up [in Berlin] he was caught smuggling his girlfriend out of the East and placed into solitary confinement for several months … Once these guys emerge from underground they see the world with different eyes.[19]

At the editing stage Herzog had valuable help from Beate Mainka-Jellinghaus, whose quick eye, independence of mind and sure taste served Kluge and Reitz as usefully as they did Herzog, from his very first feature film, *Signs of Life*, onwards. 'She was always very good', the director explained to Paul Cronin, 'at instantly sensing what was the best footage sitting in front of her', adding that she helped him to see how important it was to concentrate on what has actually been shot and not try to squeeze the footage 'into a preconceived notion that has been brought into the editing room from the original script'.[20] How well this lesson has been learnt may be seen from a comparison between Herzog's prose version of *Nosferatu* and the resulting film – including the all-important transposition of a vision of mummified corpses from near the end to the title sequence of the film, alongside a host of alterations, omissions and further transpositions.

Many of Herzog's small team, a staff consisting of some twelve people, had worked and gained qualifications outside the film industry. Henning von Gierke, the chief set designer, was joined by Ulrich Bergfelder, a scholarly connoisseur of Provençal languages and Troubadour poetry; Cornelius Siegel, mathematician and master carpenter, could construct within a couple of days a mechanical clock featuring a skull that opened on the stroke of twelve to allow a skeleton to emerge, and a figure of Time that moved across and disappeared again, as well as simpler special effects suitable for a vampire film. The elegant and beautiful Gisela Storch designed the period costumes that *Nosferatu*, like Herzog's other feature films, demanded. Claude Chiarini, a Parisian doctor and alienist who had supervised the hypnotising of actors in *Heart of Glass,* provided the still photography; and Reiko Kruk, a Japanese-born make-up expert, subjected Herzog's vampire to four hours of make-up transformation every shooting day. Many of these, along with some technicians and passing friends, also served as extras, playing small parts like that of the inspector who examines the earth and rat-filled coffins at the port of Varna; a monk praying for the dead; a man trying to mount a goat as though it were a horse; and a festively dressed group having a last meal together before dying of the plague. Herzog made sure that they all saw themselves as part of a company of friends rather than employees, ready to take a hand in any aspect of film-making without caring too much about trade-union demarcations.

And so to the actors.

Chief among them, and constantly ready to disrupt the friendly co-operative atmosphere just described, was Herzog's inspiration and the

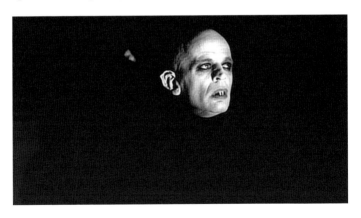

Klaus Kinski as Dracula

thorn in his side, Klaus Kinski. A stage actor, Kinski had first achieved
fame and notoriety as a reciter of poetry, specialising in German
translations and adaptations of Villon and Rimbaud, whose magnetic voice
and presence led some female members of his audience to send him
letters not unlike those Hitler received by the sack-load from German
women under his spell:

Your eyes are like mountain lakes, into which a million stars shine …
Sometimes they are like the sea when it rages wildly and the rays of the sun
create rainbows on its high waves … in all the pictures [of the world's great
painters] I see you – your eyes, your lips, your will, your power and energy…

My soul is rent, I can hardly breathe, inexpressible woe and happy, blessed
exaltation at seeing you and hearing you speak has deprived me of
utterance … I was shaken, despairing and yet unspeakably happy … My
heart bleeds, yet it is full of the infinite sweetness of the moments I was in
your presence…[21]

These and similar tributes to his magnetic personality strengthened a
streak of monomania in him, a tendency to hysteria that led to frenetic
outbursts on his later 'Jesus tours', which exerted a morbid fascination on
audiences who came to witness (and sometimes provoke) his outbursts
rather than to be edified.

    He could be sweet, considerate and affectionate to his fellow
actors, but his rages on set and off were legendary, and it needed all his
director's patience and obstinacy to coax him into a precarious
equilibrium. Kinski has had many cameo parts in German and Italian
films, and he is always mesmerising to watch; but it was Herzog who
gave him the starring roles for which he will be remembered. After *Cobra
Verde* in 1987 even Herzog's powers of endurance ran out, and he made
no further films with his 'best fiend' ('Mein liebster Feind'); but he
always knew that no one could have better embodied his conceptions of
Aguirre, Nosferatu, Wozzek or Fitzcarraldo – roles in which the
fascination Kinski could exert has been cunningly brought out alongside

the disruptive and self-destructive elements of his complex and violent personality.

While Herzog keeps the title *Nosferatu* as a homage to Murnau, he goes back to Stoker for the names of some of the principal characters. Kinski is now Dracula again, not Orlok. Lucy and Mina exchange names: the new Mina, now a friend and not Jonathan Harker's bride and later wife, is played by Herzog's own wife Martje Grohmann, who performs her much reduced part very prettily. Mina dies, as her counterpart Annie does in Murnau, without becoming a vampire herself, presumably saved from this fate by Dracula's death. The new Lucy, counterpart of Stoker's Mina and Murnau's Ellen, is played by the stage-trained French actress Isabelle Adjani, who had a partly North African (Berber) background. She had become internationally famous after Truffaut had cast her as Victor Hugo's tragic daughter in *L'Histoire d'Adèle H.* (1975), she had starred as the psychic heroine of Polanski's *Le Locataire* (*The Tenant*, 1976) and Walter Hill had used her to good effect in her Hollywood debut, *The Driver*, in 1977. Her frail beauty, huge eyes and somewhat nervous aura suggested a virginity that nevertheless gave off a strong sexual allure; Herzog therefore saw in her a predestined prey and conqueror of the male vampire more apt than the strong-minded Mina of Stoker's novel or the soulful Ellen projected by Greta Schroeder in Murnau's film. She was also wonderful at expressing terror, as in her blood-curdling cry near the opening of Herzog's film, and again in its middle; and this made Lucy's ultimate resolve to sacrifice herself by luring Dracula to her bed at once more powerful and more ambiguous. Has terror turned to sexual desire? Adjani projects both with equal force and delicacy.

Perhaps Herzog's most interesting casting is that of Roland Topor as Renfield. Topor, a French artist and writer of East European ancestry, is renowned for his disturbing drawings full of black humour and grotesque nightmare images, his absurdist plays and his long-running puppet shows on French television; his involvement with the neo-Dadaist group Panique, to which the dramatist Fernando Arrabal and the film-maker Alejandro Jodorowsky also adhered; his design for the animated film *La Planète sauvage* (1973 – domesticated in English as *Fantastic Planet*); his arresting movie

posters; and his suitably grotesque set and costume designs for revivals of earlier absurdist plays like Alfred Jarry's *Ubu Roi*. He had also written the screenplay for Polanski's *The Tenant*, which, as we have just seen, starred Adjani. He had the kind of gnome-like, somewhat disturbing presence that much of his work suggested; Herzog had watched him being interviewed on television, noted the peculiar giggling laugh that punctuated his speech and knew at once that he had found a Renfield to match that of Alexander Granach in Murnau's film. Topor died, unexpectedly, in the very year Herzog's film was released – *Nosferatu* thus became a last memorial to one of the most idiosyncratic and fascinating artists of recent times.

Roland Topor (top) as Renfield. Bruno Ganz as Jonathan and Isabelle Adjani as Lucy

The fourth most important member of Herzog's cast is the talented Bruno Ganz, an actor of Swiss origin, famous for finely nuanced performances on the German stage as well as in films directed by (among others) Eric Rohmer, Peter Handke, Wolfgang Petersen and Wim Wenders. Ganz became one of the favoured stars of the controversial theatre director Peter Zadek; his assumption of the title role in Zadek's production of *Hamlet* (1999) brought him to the attention of another innovative director, Peter Stein, and it was a filmed version of Stein's production of Gorky's *Summer Folk* (*Sommergäste*, 1976) that fired Ganz's interest in the art of film and made him into one of the icons of the New German Cinema. His closest association was with Wim Wenders, but he is also renowned for performances in films by Schlöndorff, Reinhard Hauff and the Swiss director Alain Tanner. *Nosferatu* has remained the only film he made with Herzog, who used the aura of melancholy that had made Ganz such ideal casting as Hamlet and Kleist's Prince of Homburg to project in his Jonathan

Herzog with Walter Ladengast

Harker a character more driven, complex, sick and finally demonic than the rather simple-minded adventurer of Murnau's film.

The rest of Herzog's cast includes the seventy-nine year-old German stage and film actor Walter Ladengast, who had already contributed an impressive character study to *The Enigma of Kaspar Hauser*, and who here projected an almost senile Van Helsing blinded by confidence in scientific rationality to the danger posed by the presence of Dracula in a German town, and another French actor, Jacques Dufilho. Dufilho had achieved prominence on account of his performances in Louis Malle's *Zazie dans la métro* (1960), Yves Robert's *La Guerre des boutons* (*The War of the Buttons*, 1962), and J. L. Trintignant's *Une journée bien remplie* (*A Well-filled Day*, 1973); after his appearance in *Nosferatu* he was contracted by Claude Chabrol for a part in *Le Cheval d'orgueil* (*House of Pride*, 1980). For Herzog he played, with great dignity, the captain of a ship now renamed the *Contamana* after the Peruvian city on the Ucayali River – the vessel Dracula takes over and converts into a ghost ship. Professional actors of this calibre are mingled, as was Herzog's practice, with non-professionals recruited because they represented types he needed to embody his vision. These range from the servant in the Transylvanian inn who gives Jonathan the book of vampire lore, to the gypsy storytellers who amplify that lore; they also include Herzog's wife, as we have seen, and members of his technical staff, along with a passing American friend.

Gypsies at the inn

There is never any sense of incongruity here: professionals and amateurs perform equally well in Herzog's ensemble, and the completed film shows no trace of the disruptions often caused by Kinski's volatile and unstable temperament, channelled into a performance that will ensure this most difficult (but also most talented) of actors a fame more lasting than his appearance in Edgar Wallace thrillers, Spaghetti Westerns and a host of mostly forgettable movies that include his second appearance as a vampire in Augusto Caminito's *Nosferatu in Venezia* of 1987–8. Kinski published an unreliable autobiography in 1975; an edited version appeared in English under the title *All I Need Is Love* (1988). He died in 1991.

By bringing Kinski together with actors like Bruno Ganz, Walter Ladengast and Jacques Dufilho, Herzog achieved an effect described by Elia Kazan when he contrasted the approach of 'professional' stage actors like Osgood Perkins with that of the majority of the members of his Group Theatre:

I believe I could take the kind of art Osgood Perkins exemplified – externally clear action, controlled every minute at every turn, with gestures spare yet eloquent – and blend that with the kind of acting the Group was built on: intense and truly emotional, rooted in the subconscious, therefore often surprising and shocking in its revelations. I could bring these two opposite and often conflicting traditions together, as they should be brought together.[22]

One actor in Herzog's cast did not fit into either of these categories. This was Clemens Scheitz, a little old man, eccentric to the point of disorientation, whom the director befriended, as he did many others who did not, for various reasons, quite fit into conventional society. He had already used Scheitz to excellent effect in *Kaspar Hauser* and *Stroszek*. The first scene in which this actor was to appear in *Nosferatu* fell victim to one of the few cuts 20th Century-Fox persuaded Herzog to make when they undertook to distribute the English version of the film: originally Scheitz was meant to go from house to house marking with a chalk cross those whose inhabitants had succumbed to the plague brought in by Nosferatu's rats. Herzog gives him a telling part, however, in a final scene in which, dressed in black and wearing his official top hat, he stands humbly and crookedly beside an impressive town official, who roughly orders him to arrest Van Helsing as Dracula's 'murderer' – and shows himself completely nonplussed by an order of a kind he has never had before ('I am unarmed!'), at a time when the prison warder is dead and there are no more police. His expression, when told in peremptory Prussian tones 'Do it, man – you are a town official!', is priceless. His plaintive helplessness introduces a touch of humour into the sombre conclusion of *Nosferatu* which is welcome and – it should be added – not at all unusual in Herzog's work: a humour that is never cruel, and never at the expense of the disadvantaged outsiders with whom the director always felt solidarity and sympathy.

The distinctive musical score of *Nosferatu* is the work of Florian Fricke, a classically trained pianist who founded a group called Popol Vuh – a name taken from the Mayan Book of Dreams venerated by the Quiché

Herzog with Clemens Scheitz

Indians and recently lauded by President Chavez of Venezuela as a text suffused with the same sanctity as the constitution of the state on which he based his authority. The small group of musicians that made up this group changed from time to time but always retained its reliance on a Moog synthesizer. Herzog and Fricke were friends and talked over the themes and shapes of the films on which they collaborated even before shooting had begun. The films they made together included *Kaspar Hauser*, *Aguirre*, *Heart of Glass*, *Fitzcarraldo* and *Cobra Verde* as well as *Nosferatu*. Much of Fricke's music has a liturgic feel to it: titles like *Hosianna Mantra* (1972 – a characteristic conflation of Christianity, Hinduism and Buddhism) and *Das Hohelied Salomons* (*Song of Songs*, 1975) bear witness to Popol Vuh's consciousness of this element in the group's performances, which ensures that it blends easily into Georgian religious chant and the 'Rheingold' music Herzog introduces into *Nosferatu*, along with Gounod's resounding 'Sanctus' which blasphemously accompanies the film's demonic ending.

In his interviews with Paul Cronin, Herzog is eloquent in praise of Fricke, commending especially his invention of a strange instrument called a 'choir organ', first used in the score for *Aguirre*. 'It is not real singing,' Herzog comments, in words that describe much of what also goes on in *Nosferatu*, 'nor is it completely artificial … It sits uneasily between the two.' The unease, of course, is deliberate, and earned Fricke the sobriquet 'the Morricone of horror'. 'Florian was always able,' Herzog continued:

to create music I feel helps audiences visualize something hidden in the images on screen, and in our own souls too … [his 'choir organ'] would sound just like a human choir but yet, at the same time, had a very artificial and eerie quality to it.'[23]

True to his custom of casting friends and collaborators who were not professional actors in small parts, Herzog induced Fricke to appear as a piano-player in *Signs of Life*, ensuring that not only his memorable blend of popular electronic music with classical and folk idioms, but his physical image too, would be transmitted to posterity.

4 Tribute and Transcendence

The title under which Herzog's film is known in English-speaking countries, *Nosferatu the Vampyre*, links itself, through the spelling of its key noun, to pre-Stoker vampire stories like John Polidori's Byron-inspired *The Vampyre*, and to the anonymously published long sequence of Victorian penny-dreadfuls *Varney the Vampyre*. Unlike the German and French subtitles, however – *Phantom der Nacht, fantôme de la nuit* – the English version conceals a second tribute to Murnau after the choice of *Nosferatu* for the main title: for 'Phantom' is one of the key words of the earlier film, made while Gerhart Hauptmann's novel *Phantom* (which was to serve as the basis for Murnau's next project, filmed under the same title) was making its serial way through a widely read Berlin journal. The use of 'Phantom' in the scenario and intertitles of Murnau's film takes the story out of the realm of unquestioned experience into one in which experience and hallucination become inextricably mixed, as they are in so

Henry Fuseli, *The Nightmare* (1781, Detroit Institute of the Arts)

Opening images

Jonathan's journey on foot

The vampire and his victims

Herzog's tableaux

Empty, ominous places

Revelry and the plague

Dracula's death …

… and his rebirth

many Romantic tales, from Tieck's *Der blonde Eckbert (Flaxen-haired Egbert*, 1797) to Hoffmann's *Der goldene Topf* (*Crock of Gold*, 1814). '*Phantom of the Night*' adds the sense of nightmare so important in Murnau, graphically underlined by the resemblance of the heavily disguised Max Schreck to the creature that crouches on the dreamer's bed in Henry Fuseli's painting *The Nightmare* (1781).[24]

It is consonant with this that the sequence that underlies the opening titles of Herzog's film is one of the most nightmarish in all his work, graphically signalling the return of the dead, a worldwide fear that is more responsible than any other for the long-lived dissemination of the myth of 'the undead'. The nightmare effect is produced by a travelling shot along, and up and down, a series of mummified corpses, all exhibiting an astonishing variety of gestures, some of which seem to mimic fear frozen at the moment of death. Herzog had seen these corpses, exhumed from an overcrowded cemetery, during a visit to the Mexican town of Guanajunto in the 1960s. He now went back, took the corpses out of the glass cases in which they had been displayed and carried them one by one to a wall, where he arranged them in a sequence that runs roughly from childhood to old age. Several of these mummified bodies have open mouths, suggesting that the strange chant of Popol Vuh on the soundtrack is a chant of the dead, accompanied by percussion that resembles an eerie heartbeat.

One of the mummified corpses

The close-up of one of these open-mouthed faces also recalls one of the icons of European Expressionism, Edvard Munch's *The Scream* of 1893 – an impression reinforced immediately afterwards when we hear Lucy, awakened from nightmarish sleep and seeing a bat climbing up the curtains, let out a scream that would not have disgraced Fay Wray getting her first sight of King Kong. Reference to Munch's celebrated image constitutes another way of paying tribute to the Expressionist movement that Murnau's film exemplified and furthered in a manner wholly different from the style chosen by Wiene and his scene designers in *Das Cabinet des Dr. Caligari* (*The Cabinet of Dr. Caligari*, 1919): most notably by using elements of the natural world for the creation of mood rather than the painted studio sets that were so conspicuous a feature of the earlier work. In this, as in so many other respects, Herzog followed Murnau's example, though he and his team also lavished equal care on interiors that tell us a good deal about the characters who have fashioned them and who live within them.

Prana Films, the poverty-row company that had commissioned Murnau's *Nosferatu*, cut costs wherever possible; and in order to disguise the obvious dependence on Stoker's novel, whose copyright was held by the author's widow, all the names used in *Dracula* were changed. There were no such copyright difficulties when Herzog came to make the new *Nosferatu*; he therefore reverted to the original names (except, as we have seen, for Mina and Lucy, whose names have been exchanged) while retaining many of Murnau's telescopings and other alterations of Stoker's plot. In both *Nosferatu*s the scene into which the Transylvanian vampire irrupts is not cosmopolitan London at the end of the nineteenth century, but a provincial German town in the earlier part of that century. Renfield (Murnau's Knock) merges in both films with the employer who sends Harker to Transylvania to sell a derelict German house to the vampiric Count. In both films Harker is warned at an inn against going further; in both a spectral carriage bears him to his destination; in both the accidental sight of a locket containing a portrait of his visitor's wife determines the Count to make her his principal victim. In both the Van Helsing figure is no stranger from Holland but a citizen of the same provincial German town in which all but the vampire habitually live; and though he has some knowledge of vampirism in Murnau's film, in both he is unable to work towards the Transylvanian invader's defeat. That task is shouldered by Harker's wife (Ellen in Murnau, Lucy in Herzog); she successfully vanquishes the vampire in Murnau's version by retaining him while he works his bloodsucking will on her beyond cockcrow; though she does the same thing in Herzog's film, her sacrifice – if that's what it is – is unable to prevent the spread of either vampirism or the rat-borne plague associated with it.

Murnau's film called itself a 'symphony', but it divides into five rather than four movements, each culminating at an important point in the plot:

1. A provincial German idyll, and the undertaking of a quest for profit and adventure.
2. The journey into the unknown, until the final frontier is crossed into the 'land of phantoms'.
3. The confrontation with the vampire on his own ground.
4. The race to foil the vampire's fell designs.
5. The destruction the vampire wreaks within the setting in which the film started, and his own annihilation.

Herzog preserves this structure, tightening it through the repetition of motifs (the slow-motion flight of a bat, the locket with Lucy's picture, which now appears at the beginning as well as in the fateful middle of the film), adding a doom-laden introduction and a coda depicting the birth of the new vampire after the destruction of the old. He also retains the intricate cross-cutting of the earlier *Nosferatu*, used to set up psychic connections between Lucy, Jonathan, Dracula and Renfield, and to produce a Griffithian thrill in the climactic race, by sea and land, from Transylvania to Germany.

Few scenes, however, are taken over from Murnau without Herzogian modifications. The genre-specific scene in and around the inn, for instance, where Jonathan is warned against proceeding any further, is dominated, unlike the earlier film, by the graceful movements, eloquent gestures and melodious Roma language of the band of gypsies – only momentarily arrested into frozen stillness when Jonathan reveals his destination. Dracula looms up in what is to become a ghost ship, not (as in Murnau) against the clearly visible rigging of the ship whose last survivor, the captain tied to his wheel, he is menacing, but against a blackness quite different from the blue-tinted darkness in later scenes of Herzog's film,

Mise en scène in Herzog and Murnau

which echoes the colour-tinted effects of the best Murnau versions. The deep black of the background lends an uncanny force to Nosferatu's chalk-white face and predatory hands. In Herzog's version the climactic conjunction of the doomed vampire and his willing victim in Lucy's bedroom has a heterosexual erotic power unmatched in Murnau. Herzog and his Japanese make-up expert have based their vampire's appearance on the look Murnau's team had created for Max Schreck, toning down only an ethnically suspect hooked nose[25] – but Kinski was encouraged to play *against* his mask, to make what might have seemed mere grotesque ugliness into something that could attract as well as frighten. Adjani, a sexually more attractive figure than Murnau's Greta Schroeder, responds to this admirably; and Kinski uses his voice, his magnetic eyes and the movement of his body (including the tender way in which he poses one of his elegantly moving claws on her breast while the other gently raises her nightdress) to make him an erotic presence that Schreck, with his stern, largely unmoving features, rigid and angular gestures, does not try to achieve. Here Herzog has restored an overt sexuality that Murnau had tried to tone down when he wrote the words 'Fällt weg' (deleted) against a scene his scriptwriter Galeen had sketched out:

Nosferatu raises his head. He is almost delirious with pleasure. Ellen's eyes are full of terrible fear. He must not leave like this, the Nosferatu. She winds her arms about him. He cannot resist. His head sinks down over her.[26]

Herzog's most powerful modification of Murnau's plot-line comes at the end, where he transposes into serious vein what Roman Polanski had satirically projected in his *Dance of the Vampires*. Lucy's sacrifice, which redeems Jonathan and ends the plague in Murnau, is useless in Herzog. Jonathan is the new vampire, Dracula's heir, who knows how to get rid of the communion wafers his late wife has spread around him for protection by commanding a maid to sweep 'the dust' away. He then tears the crucifix from his neck and shows the long-nailed claws and snake-like teeth inherited from a Nosferatu not reduced to smoke and ash as in Murnau's version, but blinded and painfully killed by the sun's rays before Van Helsing, convinced at last, dispatches him in the approved manner by hammering a stake through his heart. Denounced by Jonathan as the Transylvanian Count's 'murderer', Van Helsing is led off by a clueless town official towards a prison whose guardians are all dead, while Jonathan rides off, under a lowering sky over a windswept plain, wafted on by a full-throated choral 'Sanctus', into a distance where Renfield is already spreading vampirism and the plague at his late master's behest. The screen slowly fades to black as viewers reflect how little difference the loving self-sacrifice of an individual can make in such a world – except, perhaps, to the self-sacrificer herself, who is here vouchsafed an erotic experience her husband apparently failed to give her. The abrupt breaking-off of the 'Sanctus' melody on the soundtrack increases our sense of menace and unease at the dark conclusion of Herzog's film.

Murnau's world had still been that of Wagner's *Flying Dutchman*, where redemption comes through the love and self-sacrifice of a woman 'pure of heart'. Herzog's is more akin to that of Don Siegel's *Invasion of the Body Snatchers* (1955), whose ending is recalled when Lucy tries frantically to tell her fellow citizens that she knows where the evil comes from and how it can be fought, only to be told to go home, for there was nothing to be done. Herzog injects an extra turn of the screw, however. While the citizens appealed to in *Body Snatchers* at least try to save themselves by driving away, those in Herzog's film push Lucy aside as they go on ceremoniously carrying the coffins of those whom they are shortly

Van Helsing comes to dispatch the vampire

bound to join. The black-coated top-hatted coffin-bearers moving in procession are taken over from Murnau; but by having them converge from all sides instead of moving in one straight line, shooting not from above but on their own level while a Cassandra-like figure rushes from one to the other with her vain warning, Herzog gives the scene, filmed with a hand-held camera, an emotional tone and import that differs significantly from the earlier film.

The birth of a new vampire at the end of his film is one of several important additions Herzog made to the scenario of the earlier *Nosferatu*. He also added three significant dialogue scenes that would have been impossible for Murnau and his scriptwriter, because they were making a silent film whose dialogue intertitles they wanted to keep to a minimum, leaving room for a variety of documents that furthered their story in partial conformity with Stoker's novel. Three such scenes stand out in Herzog's film. The first places Jonathan and his uncanny host in a dark room fitfully lit by a few candles, where the latter explains his provenance and death-in-life state. In the second Lucy visits Renfield in his asylum cell, just before he makes his escape to join 'the Master', whose coming he announces to Lucy when she speaks of her resolve to travel to the land beyond the forest in search of her too-long-absent husband. The third shows the vampire Count intruding into the room in which Lucy stands at the mirror of her dressing-table – a turning-point of the film that will be discussed later in this study.

Herzog's physical boldness restores one effect envisaged by Murnau and his scriptwriter that had proved impossible to film. The extras playing the stevedores who stand around the earth-filled coffin opened for inspection at Varna were originally meant to have been barefoot, one of them placing his naked foot among the rats teeming within the coffin to suggest the origin of the plague. Neither Murnau's nor Herzog's players were willing to risk being bitten by these rodents – the bare foot and hand that descend into the coffin in Herzog's film are characteristically the director's own.

There are many signs, beyond the restoration of the original names, that Herzog has gone back to Stoker's *Dracula* for inspiration. A multitude of instances include the famous 'children of the night' speech, which praises

Murnau's *Nosferatu*

the 'music' they make to the accompaniment of wolves howling outside, and Dracula's speeches about the nobility of his ancestry and the 'soul of a hunter' city folk cannot understand. The main focus of his attention, however, is on Murnau; and while, as I have tried to indicate, his film is, in its different way, as admirable as Murnau's, there are moments when the latter's staging is superior. One of these is what Andreas Kilb has recently called Murnau's answer to the Lumières' *L'Arriveé d'un train en Gare de la Ciotat* (*Arrival of a Train at Ciotat Station*, 1895) and perhaps his greatest image: the entry of the vampire's ship into the harbour of the city his arrival will harm: 'The death-ship glides along like a black cloud. For the first time in the silent cinema one *hears* silence, the dying away of every sound. No later horror film has ever outdone the horror of this first image.'[27] What Kilb fails to point out is that in Murnau's version the dark sails blot from our sight the German city's church; the sails of Herzog's *Contamana* do so only intermittently, disrupting the symbolic effect. Another such moment is the wide-eyed gaze of the vampiric outsider about to penetrate into the deepest human interior. As Murnau's vampire Count stands at a ruined window divided into nine glassless sections, his head and differently clawing hands each occupy one small frame, while his intensely staring eyes and coiled stance convey a frightening impression of a monster about to take his final spring. Here, for once, Kinski is less effectively presented – his gaze lacks Schreck's intensity, his hands are not as powerfully disposed, the window is less impressively divided and his ascent to Lucy's bedroom lacks the uncanny shadow-play with which Murnau bridges the sequence of the ultimate gaze and that of the ultimate penetration.

In his commentary on his own film, recorded on the DVD listed at the end of the Select Bibliography, Herzog has freely admitted that in this instance he has lagged behind his great predecessor. The admission does him credit, but it should not be allowed to obscure the extent to which he achieved his principal object: that of paying due tribute to a master and the tradition he represented, while transcending it in a recognisably 'Herzogian' film redolent of personal experience and the worldview crystallised out of it.

5 Nobodaddy's Universe

In adult life, his youthful Catholicism behind him, Herzog retained a
strong interest in religious ceremony and (often extreme) signs of
devotion. His quarrel with his father, however, and with the generation of
fathers that voted in and supported a barbarous regime, has a mirror
image in the argument with God that runs through much of his work. The
German title of his film about the famous foundling Kaspar Hauser
proclaims that every man is for himself and God is against all – *Jeder für
sich und Gott gegen alle* – while the title of his film about the Spanish
conquistadores speaks of Aguirre as 'the wrath of God'. This metaphysical
framework is patent in *Nosferatu*. According to the old book from which
Jonathan and Lucy learn vampire lore in the teeth of Van Helsing's
scientific rationality, the vampire is said to be 'of the seed of Belial' – a
being proclaimed the enemy of Christ in II Corinthians 6:15, and one of
Satan's counsellors in *Paradise Lost*. Lucy proclaims that a love such as she
feels for Jonathan 'even God cannot alter'; and when her friend Mina
seeks to allay her anxiety with a conventional 'the Lord will hear our
prayers', Lucy answers: 'God is so far from us in the hour of our distress' –
in direct contradiction of the belief that prayer brings us nearer to God
and that he 'hears' us. As so often happens, however, such disavowals do
not prevent Lucy from praying, as she scatters crumbs from consecrated
wafers over the earth in Dracula's coffin, that she may be forgiven this
sacrilege. It is Lucy who enunciates the sense of 'an inner, nameless,
deadly fear' that pervades the film, in which demons seem to rule instead
of God: a theme that comes to a head when Renfield says to his master
Dracula 'Thy will be done' (adding 'Amen' to drive home the idea of
'perverted religion') and when a chorus proclaiming God's holiness, from
a mass by Gounod, ironically accompanies the vampire's wild ride at the
end of the film.

One important change made by Galeen and Murnau was the transfer
of their vampire story from Stoker's metropolitan London to a provincial
German city, and the shift from Stoker's (for him contemporary) late
Victorian period to an earlier one. Their chronicler places the great plague

associated with the arrival of the Nosferatu from Transylvania in the year 1843. This puts it at the heart of an epoch that was being re-evaluated by art historians and critics of literature during the course of the Weimar Republic: the Biedermeier.[28] After initial ridicule this had become, for many Germans, a source of nostalgia for an idyllic provincial life that had existed before the advent of the railways and the industrial revolutions, attested by the popularity of such artists as Karl Spitzweg.

It was increasingly recognised, however, that the idyll was menaced; that political and social forces were at work in the period that followed the end of the Napoleonic wars which would erupt in the revolutions of 1848. Revaluations of the work of writers like Adalbert Stifter, Franz Grillparzer and Eduard Mörike detected a sense of the precariousness of the balance that was being maintained, and of the coexistence of ideas deriving from French and British sources that threatened an ideal Thomas Mann once called 'machtgeschützte Innerlichkeit' – the inwardness of citizens unconcerned with politics and protected by a powerful establishment. That somewhat mitigated the distance Murnau's film set between its storyline and its first intended audiences, who yearned for a more idyllic existence. It should be remembered here that earlier films like *The Cabinet of Dr. Caligari* and *Der Student von Prag* (*The Student of Prague*, 1913) had been set in the same period, which was felt to belong, not only to the threatened Biedermeier idyll but also to 'Dark Romanticism' in the person of E. T. A. Hoffmann, who had lived on until 1822, and whose tales had never lost their fascination – especially since Freud had used Hoffmann as a principal exhibit in his essay on 'The Uncanny', published in 1919, the year of *Caligari*.

Herzog's decision to retain Murnau's Biedermeier setting, with its suggestion of an idyll disrupted from within as well as without, has an additional force in his film when one remembers that the Federal Republic of the 'economic miracle' years was often termed 'the new Biedermeier' by those who castigated the cult of private enrichment and material comfort in what in Britain was called the 'I'm All Right, Jack' spirit. But more and more historians and cultural analysts were pointing out that *Angst* was never far from the original Biedermeier; and the memory of what had been done in

Germany's name only a few years earlier, and what had happened to many Germans during the final stages and after the collapse of an evil regime, might well connect with the Cold War and the violent activities of the Baader–Meinhof Gang and others, to lend topicality to the theme of the 'threatened idyll' in the newly prosperous second Biedermeier of the Federal Republic – whose citizen Herzog always remained.

Futility, anxiety and existential danger are often signalled in Herzog's films by images of circular movement found in *Signs of Life*, *Auch Zwerge haben klein angefangen* (*Even Dwarves Started Small*, 1970), *Stroszek* and in some documentaries – even in the devotional context of his film about Buddhist pilgrimages and ceremonies, *Wheel of Time*. In *Wheel of Time* it

Wheeling vessels

takes the form of a monkey held on a string, forced to turn one somersault after another to attract alms to a beggar – a particularly ironic glimpse in a film devoted to a religion that insists on respect for all forms of life. In *Nosferatu* it is Jonathan Harker who first brings the image to mind when he tells Renfield, his employer, that he will be glad to make a journey that may cost him not only a lot of time and effort but also, as Renfield says with a sinister giggle, 'a little blood'. He will be glad because it will take him out of a town full of canals that lead nowhere but back to themselves. Visually the image is suggested again in the wheeling motions of first the raft, then the ship, carrying death and destruction to Wismar and rendering void Jonathan's hopes of bringing back prosperity for himself and his wife; and it governs the overall form of the film in which Jonathan's ride out of Wismar at the beginning is echoed by his very different ride at the end.

The anxiety that pervades this film from the very beginning is reinforced by Herzog's strengthening of the suggestions inherent in the German title that characterises Nosferatu as a 'Phantom of the Night'. Herzog's protagonists ask themselves and others whether they are not in a dream or nightmare; and when Lucy asks Van Helsing, in words adapted from Stoker, whether they were not all suffering from insane delusions and will wake up to find themselves in straitjackets, we seem to be entering *Caligari* country. The shot, repeated at significant intervals, of a castle ruin on a mountain top is clearly *not* the inhabitable edifice in which

The ruined castle

Dracula entertains his victim, yet the placing of the image suggests that they are identical. This reinforces what the gypsies tell Jonathan when they warn him against going any further: there is no such castle in the 'real' world; it exists only in the imagination of men who penetrate to a region where 'the light divides' – one part going up, the other down. This points again to a Manichaean worldview in which we look up to an infinitely remote God who is even, as *Kaspar Hauser* had suggested, 'against all', and feel that in the world of delusion down below, the seed of Belial is allowed to rage in the form of a Nosferatu who lords it over plague-bearing rats – a conjunction that would remind every educated German of Mephisto in Goethe's *Faust*, who is, among other things, 'Herr der Ratten'. This is a conjunction Herzog has taken over from Murnau's *Nosferatu*, which Murnau followed shortly afterwards, first by the film actually entitled *Phantom* (1992) and later by his own version of *Faust*.

Metaphysical evil, then, is at work in a world in which the Christian symbols liberally employed to combat it – crucifixes, Eucharistic wafers, holy water, the sign of the cross made over forehead and chest – are ultimately shown to have been powerless. The findings of science, however, are shown to be no less so. In Herzog's film Van Helsing has only scientific interests in common with his original in Stoker, who combined these with a deep learning in occult lore that enabled him to vanquish the vampire and help to re-establish order in the Victorian society Dracula tried to invade and disrupt. Even the ineffective Bulwer of Murnau's film has insights derived from his study of Paracelsus (who had investigated the medical uses of chemicals and minerals, along with the effects of laudanum, against a background of mystical hopes and alchemical expectations). Bulwer's study of vampirism in nature induces belief in vampiric powers, but provides him with no weapons to combat them; in the end it is only 'a woman of pure heart' who is able to vanquish evil as effectively as Stoker's stakes and decapitations. Not so in Herzog's darker film: as Lucy's tender gesture ensures one Nosferatu's destruction, the second is already waiting in the adjoining room.

The gypsies, whom Herzog presents with evident sympathy, are the main spokesmen of the 'Phantom' view announced by the film's German

title. Some of them, the landlord of the inn explains, have 'been to the other side' and experienced a darkness that is more than just the absence of light. Jonathan ignores their warnings against the perils and delusions that await him if he proceeds, just as he fails to heed what he reads in the Book of Vampires he is given at the inn; but even as he sets out to continue his journey in bright daylight, the phantom phenomenon asserts itself. The coachman from whom Jonathan demands transport stands in front of what we are shown to be a carriage with a team of horses tethered to it, but he denies what we and Jonathan think we are seeing: 'There is no carriage', 'I have no horses', 'there is no path'. The cinema, with its two-dimensional simulacrum of our three-dimensional world, is of course

A ring of holy wafers

peculiarly well fitted to convey such 'phantom' suggestions; indeed, early German cinema made prominent use of such an effect, as Herzog, deliberately harking back to its Expressionist phase, does also in this second *Nosferatu*.

Dracula's castle, the gypsies explain to Jonathan, exists only in men's imaginations. A possible reading, therefore, suggests that everything we see happening after Jonathan's departure from Wismar may be his delusion – as Jonathan himself, in his letter to Lucy, seems to suspect. This would make Dracula the projection of his apparent victim, who has felt stifled among the canals of his day-to-day life and dissatisfied with the sexual aspect of his relations with his frightened doe of a wife – a dissatisfaction suggested by the suspicious haste with which he leaves her in the opening breakfast scene (for which she admonishes him) and his readiness to go on an expedition among 'wolves, robbers and ghosts' in order, as he rationalises it, to buy her a better house. Such rationalisations are as well known to psychologists as the takeover of the conscious by the repressed part of the personality when, after Nosferatu has consummated a pseudo-marriage with a partner who is now safely dead, Jonathan himself *becomes* Nosferatu. Such are the delusions possible in a world in which God is infinitely remote or even hostile to mankind. As Novalis has said: 'Where there are no gods, spectres hold sway' ('Wo keine Götter sind, walten Gespenster').

6 Melancholy Vampire

Whether we think of Herzog's Dracula as a projection of Jonathan's hidden self or not, he is a sufficiently interesting figure to warrant a closer look than has been possible so far. It is, of course, well known that the film-makers who have bent Stoker's creation to their own purposes have presented him in two guises: as a courtly, fashionably or ceremonially dressed, but nonetheless dangerous, being (portrayed by Bela Lugosi, Christopher Lee, Ferdy Mayne, Frank Langella and various others inside and outside the English-speaking world); or as a being frightful to look at and equally frightful in action (Max Schreck, Willem Dafoe – reasonably handsome actors both, frighteningly made up).

It has been said that both of these portrayals were anticipated by Stoker, the first exemplified by Dracula in his Transylvanian domain, the second by Dracula in London and Wismar. This is hardly tenable, however, for despite some feral characteristics that are never shed (hairy palms, pointed ears, sharp teeth), the Transylvanian Dracula is a dignified, white moustached old aristocrat, conscious of a heroic past and ancestry, who only shows his true nature when he attacks Jonathan Harker – thundering 'This man is mine!' at the three female vampires who try to anticipate the feast of blood he had reserved for himself. The one fundamental change in his appearance and demeanour once he has settled

Bela Lugosi in *Dracula* (Tod Browning / Universal Pictures, 1931)

into England with its many tempting throats is that he is progressively rejuvenated by the increasing quantity of blood he is able to consume. In Herzog's film Kinski's make-up is based on that of Max Schreck; but though physically the two Nosferatus resemble one another, morally and spiritually they are worlds apart. Herzog has been accused of sentimentalising Murnau's now world-famous conception. I yield to no one in my admiration of Murnau and Schreck, but would argue that both conceptions are equally valid as film-specific reinterpretations of the figure Stoker had introduced into Victorian literature and modern mythology.

The vampire of Murnau's film is soulless: he is driven by his physical need to sustain his 'undead' Nosferatu state by ingesting the blood of the

Roman Polanski in *Dance of the Vampires* (Roman Polanski / Cadre Films, Filmways Motion Pictures, 1967)

Frank Langella in *Dracula* (John Badham / Mirisch, Universal Pictures, 1979)

living, and by a vestige of sexuality that makes him eager to feast on a 'beautiful neck'. Herzog's vampire, however, lets us into his inner life sufficiently to know that he has retained a suffering soul through his many years of 'undead' existence. He is, of course, driven by his need for blood, like all vampires; but we see him actually struggling against this compulsion endemic in what he calls, with Stoker, his 'soul of a hunter', when he tries to resist the urge to pounce on the blood oozing from Jonathan's finger after the latter has accidentally cut himself – only to succumb to the need implanted in him.

In the long conversation with Jonathan, held in a room where a few candles seem only to deepen the darkness out of which looms the dead-white, infinitely sad face of a vampire weary of his existence, Herzog's Dracula gives us something like a compendium of existential anguish prolonged beyond that of mortal men. Cast into an abyss of time, 'a thousand nights deep', he is forced to experience centuries of *Nichtigkeiten* (futilities), that recall the world of meaningless gossip and empty impersonality into which Heidegger saw humankind *geworfen*, 'flung'. Out of this existential anguish, expressed not only in words but in the half-suppressed moans he emits throughout his appearances in Herzog's film, he seeks the escape he proposes to Lucy after surprising her before a mirror in which he casts a shadow but no reflection. If he could partake of the love between Lucy and Jonathan by drawing them into his deathless world, they might together attain an equivalent of the meaningfulness, the authenticity, human beings achieve in confrontations with fully experienced love and with the accepted fact of death.

When Lucy rejects him, achieving her own form of authenticity by growing from a frightened child to a determined woman who knows the course she must follow, Dracula has his revenge by forcing his alter ego Jonathan into the same futile and destructive mode of being he had himself sought to escape. And strangely enough, as the burden is shifted onto Jonathan, Dracula actually *finds* that escape. His ultimate encounter with Lucy is a night of love, on a bed strewn with rose petals, signs of tenderness and orgiastic sighs emitting from both partners; and the death he dies is not the dissolution into a puff of smoke, like Murnau's Orlok, but an authentically human death, with blindness, convulsion, pain and an indrawing of breath as though sucking what Rilke called a 'great death' into himself. The subsequent 'staking' by Van Helsing is shoved off-screen; it fulfils one of the requirements of the vampire genre, but it also allows Herzog's Jonathan to accuse someone else of 'murdering' the alter ego that had taken his place in sexually satisfying a wife he himself had deserted and no longer even recognised after his vain expedition to the land 'beyond the forest'. Such projections of guilt, and covert recognitions of failure, involve psychological mechanisms that have inspired many a *Doppelgänger* tale and are all too common in human experience.

If one sees Dracula as a *Doppelgänger*, a projection of Jonathan's hidden self, Herzog's presentation of a Transylvanian vampire filled with German *Sehnsucht* (romantic longings for a more authentic mode of being), and an existential *Angst* that takes an equally German (Heideggerian rather than Sartrean) form, falls easily into place. His Dracula becomes a voice that whispers secrets of the soul. Herzog has told many times how he compelled Kinski, who wanted to play a tyrant in Bottom's vein ('a part to tear a cat in') to use his softest, most seductive mode of speaking. He let the actor shout and rage, threatening the director and anyone else who crossed him with physical violence, until he had become hoarse, quiet and dangerous – and only then were the cameras allowed to roll. Kinski was no fool; he knew full well that Herzog was not only forcing him to embody a very particular conception of Dracula, but that he was once again bringing out qualities in Kinski himself that other directors had ignored but which were likely to ensure his lasting fame.

What Dracula's longing for death as one escape from the 'futilities' of his existence (the other, of course, is a human form of love) in fact implies is enunciated by a man who is taking part in a last formal supper party in the midst of the chaos of a plague-stricken city. He invites the distraught Lucy to join them: 'be our guest', he says. 'This is our last supper. We have all caught the plague. *For the first time in our lives we rejoice at every day we have left.*' The theological reference is ironic, for we know that no resurrection is likely to follow; what matters, however, is the

Longing for death

characteristically existentialist affirmation of a life lived authentically in the consciousness, not that all men are mortal, but that each must face his own particular death.

In Stoker's novel, it is interesting to recall, Dracula is also heard occasionally to speculate on what a great experience death might be, and Van Helsing attributes this to a longing to escape a vampiric existence. His rationale, however, is notably different: 'That poor soul who has wrought all this misery', he says of Dracula, 'is the saddest case of all. Just think what will be his joy when he too is destroyed in his worser part that his better part may have spiritual immortality.'[29] The only 'immortality' Herzog's Dracula achieves, after Lucy has helped him escape the 'futilities' of his existence and Van Helsing has completed the process in the way the genre demands, is that of passing on to another that 'soul of a hunter' he himself had come to loathe. Van Helsing's metaphysical certainties are foreign to Herzog's film.

So far, my reading has given pride of place to Jonathan, seeing Dracula, Lucy and Van Helsing as all part of one mind trying to cope with its nightmares, slipping into different personages at different times, seeking ways of dealing with what it experiences. It is easy to find Jungian terms for all this: Shadow, Anima, Counsellor ... But our experience in the cinema is not quite like that. We appear to be slipping in and out of Jonathan's world, into that of Dracula, then Lucy's, sharing modes of apprehensions that are different from our own, yet seem to have a connection with them. There is no controlling narrator, like the chronicler of Murnau's film, no ordering consciousness, slotting everything into place, like Stoker's Mina Harker. Herzog's 'Phantom of the Night' transports us into German Romantic territory again, Tieck's *Flaxen-haired Egbert*, Hoffman's *Devil's Elixirs*, whose uncertainties speak to us of our own, raising apprehensions that are, to use Edgar Allan Poe's phrase, 'not of Germany, but of the soul'.

As the new Nosferatu, Dracula's ultimate heir, Bruno Ganz does not have anything like the charisma of Kinski; but he is an excellent actor who conveys convincingly all the changes Herzog's screenplay demands of him. From the concerned husband who slips into his wife's bed only to soothe her fears, with a tender embrace that has nothing overtly sexual in it, he becomes the embodiment of a go-ahead entrepreneur who gladly executes a dangerous journey not only for profit but to escape the confinement of the house he leaves in such haste and the town whose canals only lead back to themselves. In a land where inner and outer merge and nothing is as it seems, he becomes a feverish, delirious being, ostensibly seeking to avert the dangers to his wife that are carried in the 'black coffins' of which he burbles, only to arrive home unable even to recognise his own wife, seeking shelter from sunlight in dark corners and behind drawn blinds. Now humming, now laughing eerily to himself, he watches as his wife becomes a bride of the alter ego he had encountered in that world of illusion beyond the forest; when the vampire and his intended victim have both died in a parodic semblance of *Liebestod*, he sheds his languor and vigorously assumes the role hitherto played by Dracula, his phantom double, now discarded along with the wife he no longer recognised.

As spectators in the cinema we may have been sharing the delusions of a deeply disturbed individual; but we have also watched a parable, told in powerful images by a great film-maker, of delusion, evil, agony, desire and occasional ecstasy in a world that has to make do without the guidance of a benevolent God. It is a parable, moreover, that brings together, in the figure of Nosferatu, the two representative characters that pervade Herzog's earlier works: outsiders in a society where they can

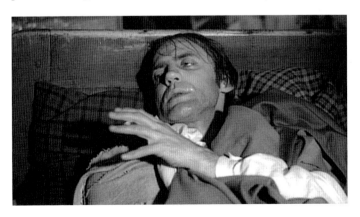

Jonathan's fever

never feel at home, and which in the end destroys them; and rebels who try, by violent means, to realise what their lives refuse them, but also ultimately fail. Kaspar Hauser is the most prominent example of the first kind; the dwarves who 'started small', Stroszek in *Signs of Life* and Aguirre, who seeks to execute the 'wrath of God', exemplify the second.

Nosferatu belongs to both camps: he is the ultimate outsider, hunted down by the world he longs to become part of; he is also, however, the rebel who brings with him the means of striking out at a world in which death is the best he can hope for. In achieving such a death in the course of a night that brings him a measure of ecstasy and a morning that releases him from a loathed immortality, he achieves a kind of triumph denied to Kaspar, assassinated by some agency he never gets to know for a purpose neither he nor we can understand; and denied to Aguirre too, who ends up on his circling raft without having achieved any of the conquests he has striven for so strenuously. In this respect he resembles Fitzcarraldo, who fails in his greater object but achieves a triumph of sorts when he brings his beloved Grand Opera to places that had not experienced it before.

The logic of Herzog's vampire parable may explain why, when he chose to restore the names Stoker had given his characters after Galeen and Murnau had disguised them for copyright reasons, he should have chosen to give Jonathan's wife and Dracula's chosen victim the name 'Lucy' while her friend is now called Mina. Stoker's Lucy is a more sexually vulnerable character than his Mina, and it is precisely that quality of sexual receptiveness that is so important to the climax of Herzog's film, in which Lucy's surrender to Dracula, intended as a sacrifice, seems to be her moment of greatest satisfaction. Under Herzog's direction Isabelle Adjani matches Kinski's performance, passing from frightened child whose terrors have to be soothed by a husband who acts more like a father, to ominous visionary no one is willing to believe, to resolute young woman determined to shoulder a task none of the males seems capable of performing: namely, defeating the vampire in an act that seems to involve a sexual surrender. The look of peace on her face after she dies, orgiastically, together with the released vampire, contrasts wonderfully

Lucy's transition

with the wide-eyed anguish she had projected so well in the earlier part of the film.

Herzog's film has been released in English and French as well as German. My study of his Nosferatu racked by existential anguish and romantic longings should demonstrate why Herzog thought the German version the most authentic, underlining the paradox that his first international co-production, employing French as well as German actors in leading parts and inducing 20th Century-Fox to ensure its distribution in English-speaking markets, is so indelibly German. Nor should this be surprising: for *Nosferatu – Phantom der Nacht* represents a deliberate attempt, even under its toned-down title *Nosferatu the Vampyre*, not just at making a film in a specific genre, but at playing distinctive variations on the Expressionist tradition of German film-making represented and developed by Murnau. As Herzog did so, he also drew on energies derived from the Romantics in Murnau's past and his own, from Wagner, and from a German variety of existentialism felt by many of his contemporaries in the Federal Republic to articulate their own feelings about the world in which they found themselves. As Elaine Showalter has said: 'There is always a reason why a country has vampire trouble, and each era has offered its own rationale for the children of the night.'[30]

7 Mysterious Journey

When Herzog's Jonathan, unlike his counterpart in Murnau's film, is denied a carriage and horses to take him, if not to Dracula's castle, at least to the frontier of the vampiric Count's domain where a phantom carriage can come to meet him, he sets out, resolutely, on foot; the sequence that follows is one of the most impressive in the whole work.

The *Fussreise* (journey on foot) has a long tradition in German life, from the journeymen who wandered from region to region between the end of their original apprenticeship and their advance to master status, to the *Wandervogel* movement of idealistic young people in the 1920s and early 30s – hijacked, in the end, along with so much else, by the Nazi youth organisations. It has a tradition in German literature too, from J. G. Seume's *Spaziergang nach Syrakus* (*A Walk to Syracuse*, 1803), Joseph von Eichendorff's *Aus dem Leben eines Taugenichts* (*Episodes from the Life of a Ne'er-do-well*, 1826) and Mörike's 'Fussreise', congenially set by Hugo Wolf, to Herzog's own *Vom Gehen im Eis* (*Walking on Ice,* 1978); in German art, with drawings and paintings by Ludwig Richter and Karl Spitzweg; and in German music, from folk song to Schubert's settings of Wilhelm Müller's poems in *The Fair Maid of the Mill* (1823) and *Winter Journey* (1827).

Herzog, who once braved midwinter to walk from Munich to Paris to visit the ailing Lotte Eisner and incidentally find a market for one of his films, has often spoken of the importance he attached to *walking*: 'I would rather do the existentially essential [!] things in my life on foot'; 'My voyages on foot have always been essential experiences for me'; 'When you come on foot, you come with a different intensity'.[31] He explained what this meant to his film-making in an interview recorded for the DVD release of *Nosferatu*, where he called it 'athletic work', describing how he needed to experience with his body the space that would be occupied by his fictional characters, to walk through every terrain he would ask his cameraman to photograph from a specific viewpoint.

It is this kind of body experience that Jonathan replicates as he sets out on foot over sunlit meadows to enter a dark and narrow ravine, with precipitous rocks on one side and torrential waters on the other; ascend from there to a desolate scene littered with huge boulders, and occasional traces of snow in a darkening world, to reach at last the summit of mountains he had earlier seen in the blue distance. We watch as he sits beside a slim flagstaff some lost explorer had planted there – or is it a marker to show that Dracula's realm extends to that point? The camera comes up behind him, showing him as a dark silhouette on an equally silhouetted mountain peak, seen from the back like a figure in a painting by Caspar David Friedrich, gazing into the distance. For a moment that distance seems to hold a promise of light beyond, as is so often the case in Friedrich's paintings; but then the camera pans away to Jonathan's right, to the mountain range overhung by moving clouds that make the screen darker and darker.

There follows a haunting sequence in which Jonathan makes his way through a tunnel-like ravine traversed by rushing waters, preceded by his huge shadow cast by the setting sun whose last rays strike the tunnel's entrance behind him. It is here that the phantom carriage – a hearse in Herzog's version – overtakes him to bear him to Dracula's castle and the fate that awaits him there. While some of this was filmed in the Tatra mountains, near the Czech–Polish border, a good deal of this dramatic footage has a special meaning for Herzog, as he filmed it near the Bavarian village in which he spent much of his youth. We do not need to

A darkening world

know this, however, to sense that what this deliberately slow *Fussreise* sequence charts is as much an inner as an outer journey; that the landscape carries the kind of meaning Novalis pointed to when he said that man's mysterious journey leads inwards: ('nach innen geht der geheimnisvolle Weg'). Wagner's 'Rheingold' prelude, superseding for a moment the chantings of Popol Vuh, helps to establish the mood of this key sequence of Herzog's film, in which the landscape speaks for the soul.

Townscapes and the interiors of human dwellings are used to similar expressive and symbolic effect. The town of Delft, with its beautiful old houses and echoes of Vermeer, is as much a character in *Nosferatu* as the corridors and staircases of Dracula's castle, where Jonathan at first

Jonathan's descent to Dracula's crypt

explores only the upper regions, but is then driven, by an increasing number of locked doors, to descend into its darkest depths, to find Dracula lying in his coffin, his eyes wide open, appearing to look straight up at the explorer. It would be hard to find a more powerful symbol for a descent into the unconscious and confrontation with an Id, a Shadow, a sinister alter ego or double. The Dutch waterways where much of the action was filmed prove similarly resonant. There are bridges to cross, on one of the first of which stands a mysterious black figure; there are reflections that add ghostly doubles to Lucy sleepwalking along the canal and to the carriage traversing a causeway that brings Jonathan to his

The ingenious clock

disastrous homecoming. The windmills seen on that journey, as with the arrival of the *Contamana* at the Wismar quayside, suggest another instance of that circular motion whose presence in Herzog's films has already been discussed. A good deal of credit for the resonance of these and other images is due to Schmidt-Reitwein's masterly camerawork, with its subtle gradations of light and dark, its chiaroscuro traversed by lengthening shadows, its catching of evanescent glimmerings on dark waters, its use of hand-held cameras to propel us into the middle of an action, its panning along a rapidly moving object like a coach and horses while also keeping its watery *Doppelgänger* firmly in focus. The outer world is there, in all its particularity – but its relevance to an inner world of human experience is never in doubt.

The *Fussreise* passage ends at Dracula's castle, whose self-opening doors and self-closing coffins echo similar effects in Murnau. It is remarkable, however, how little camera trickery there is in *Nosferatu* (as in other Herzog films). There are no computer-generated effects, no Schüfftan processes or imposition of matte-paintings on a photographed landscape or building. What special effects there are are really *bricolage*, like the ingenious clock constructed by Cornelius Siegel, whose midnight chime startles Jonathan and leads him to cut his finger. The recurrent slow-motion bat has been taken from some scientific documentary, like the Venus flytrap and polyp in Murnau's film – but Herzog does reserve one startlingly effective camera trick for the very end. As Jonathan rides across the swiftly shifting sands of a windswept plain towards a distant horizon, dark clouds descend lower and lower – these are thunderclouds *whose photographed image has been inverted*, creating a more and more threatening mood as we lose sight of the death-dealing rider and the screen fades to black.

Like Murnau and many other great film-makers, Herzog is keenly aware of how contrast can heighten the power of the mysterious journey on which he asks his spectators to accompany the characters of his story. At the very beginning of the film the open-mouthed gesturing corpses and Lucy's cry on awakening from 'yet another nightmare' is followed by the idyllic scene of kittens playing among decoratively arranged fruit and

Murnau's found footage

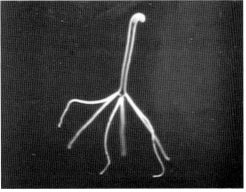

books, and shots of a tranquil town with bridges over quiet waters. This movement is reversed almost immediately: from the bright breakfast room with its beautiful flowers we pass along a pleasant quayside walk, encountering leisurely people in mild sunlight, to the darkness of Renfield's inner office, where a sinister messenger relays Dracula's fateful command. Here the contrast also involves order and disorder, as we pass from the pellucidly arranged breakfast room, with its flowers, its bright crockery on a well-laid table, its well-bound books, a sideboard displaying patterned plates, and symmetrically hung pictures, to Renfield's office, with its welter of documents crammed higgledy-piggledy on overfilled shelves – they appear to have been pushed in wherever there might just be a tiny space for them, and no one but (perhaps) the pathetic clerk, who seems to be an immemorial part of the general disorder, could ever find his way about such chaos.

The order/disorder contrast is also evident, of course, in the behaviour of Wismar's citizens before the plague hits their town, and the dancing, goat-mounting, rat-dangling amidst straying beasts, abandoned furniture and ubiquitous rats that we see afterwards. Here, however, Herzog introduces one of his most characteristic touches. Another director (Cecil B. De Mille, perhaps?) might have introduced an orgy at this point, and some critics have expressed disappointment in this scene, where sexual desire is expressed through dance (the man with the goat seems to be trying to ride it rather than satisfying himself some other way). However, Herzog does something more unusual by showing beautifully dressed people (played mainly by members of his technical team) attempting one last time to maintain civilised values around a festive table, while plague-bearing rats swarm about their feet, and a nearby table, which might have been laid for just such a purpose, has already been overrun by rodents. I find this self-assertion of humanity in the face of the gruesome death that awaits it particularly moving. That one participant speaks of this feast as the company's 'Last Supper' introduces an ironic resonance into this scene that deepens our sense of the absence, remoteness or hostility of God.

A last meal in a time of plague

Jonathan's journey on foot towards his encounter with Dracula involves more than just a passage from light to dark – from the sunlit meadow in which the walk begins to the gathering darkness of the mountain peak and the gloom of the ravine in which the phantom carriage overtakes the wanderer; it is also a passage from the bright colours of the wayside inn, and the many-hued costumes of the gypsies, to the greys and blacks of the mountain landscape, fitfully traversed by the whiteness of agitated waters and waterfalls, and a few ragged patches of snow. Jonathan's ochre travelling-coat offsets the black costume of the (artificially heightened) form of Kinski's Dracula at the castle gate; and that, in its turn, will contrast significantly with the white clothing in which Lucy so often appears – offset by bright red sleeves in the sequence that precedes her final white-on-black encounter with the vampire. That conjunction had, of course, become canonical in terror films, ever since black-clad Cesare abducted white-gowned Jane in *The Cabinet of Dr. Caligari.*

The pattern of contrasts applies to movement too. Jonathan's slow ascent is framed between his earlier rides on horseback and later swift drive in the phantom carriage sent to meet him. When we first see Dracula, his movements are slow and stately, and they remain so for most of the film, even slowing down with uncanny effect when Dracula approaches Jonathan's bed in the castle and Lucy asleep in her home; but it can also speed up disconcertingly, as when Dracula pounces on Jonathan's cut finger, when he hastily loads coffins for his journey onto a cart, or when he sprints across a dark town square in Wismar to reach the safety of his coffin before dawn. In these nocturnal Wismar scenes darkness has a blue *virage* effect that it did not possess before: a contrast between dark and dark supplementing that between dark and light already described.

Several other traits of Herzog's film-making are well illustrated by Jonathan's enforced journey on foot. The first is his predilection for showing characters from behind – especially at moments of great emotion – so that we have to work out for ourselves what their feelings are instead

Filming from behind

of having them presented in huge close-ups of tearful, joyful or agitated faces. We see this when Jonathan and Lucy prepare for their leave-taking by walking beside a calm sea, or when Lucy sits among graves looking out beyond the waves she expects will bring Jonathan back to her; and here it is again, as Jonathan rests on the summit of the mountain he has just ascended and gazes across to what he will experience as Dracula's castle, but what we may see as the uninhabitable ruin of which the gypsies have spoken and that is twice shown us from afar as very different from the Pernstein Castle in Moravia in which many of the interior scenes were filmed. We may also recall once again that black-clad figure on the bridge that appeared near the opening of the film, reminding us of Herzog's way of introducing silent figures, who while taking no part in the action, deepen or modify a mood. The violin-scraping gypsy boy who appears and disappears so mysteriously at salient points of Jonathan's stay in Dracula's castle is another example, as are the silent onlookers who are present when the *Contamana*'s dead captain is discovered and the ship's log is removed, representing the many who will die as a result of the ship's sinister cargo.

A particularly charming presence among these onlookers is the little girl whom the camera picks out at the side of the canal where the ghost ship, its dead captain clearly visible slumped over his wheel, has been

Onlookers

anchored. She sneezes twice, at which point many will remember the commonly held superstition that a sneeze might herald the plague, and that the sneezer should therefore be wished good health (*Gesundheit*) or given a blessing. Such conjunctions of the charmingly innocent and the ominous – the pretty little girl, the dead captain, the plague-bearing ship – are of course, at the very heart of Herzog's film.

The shot of Jonathan resting on the mountain top amidst the gathering clouds also reminds us of Herzog's liking for occasionally arresting the forward thrust of his narrative by freezing his characters for a moment into a tableau: Renfield straining within his straitjacket flanked by two warders, all three side by side, facing the camera as in a period photograph; a wistful Lucy sitting at her window yearning for Jonathan's return, as in a picture by a Romantic painter like G. F. Kersting; the two old people in Jonathan's sick-room who sit quietly next to each other until the old woman joins a gypsy and a nursing sister in trying to prevent a feverish Jonathan leaving his sick-bed to save a wife he will no longer recognise when at last he reaches what had been his home.

Just as Herzog likes occasionally to arrest the forward motion that is the *raison d'être* of the cinema in order to approach the stasis of a still photograph or a painting, so he also likes to deprive audiences of the sounds that they have come to expect ever since Al Jolson spoke and sung those first words on the world's screens. When Lucy strays into the

disordered marketplace in which animals and men commingle under the
impact of the plague, we see a man blowing his horn but do not hear him,
we see people dancing and speaking, but cannot hear what they are saying
– an uncanny effect not broken until we come to the table at which elegant
people, knowing they are doomed, choose to create their brief moment of
order. Such deprivations of sound sometimes put us on a par with a
character on the screen. A striking instance occurs when Dracula,
preceded by his huge shadow cast by streetlamps, stands vigil outside
Jonathan's house. As his dark presence looms up, seen from the back and
momentarily in profile we observe with him the scene within the house:
the sick Jonathan sitting close to the window in the middle ground,
isolated from the figures further back – Lucy, Van Helsing, Mina and her
husband. Like the watcher at the window, we guess at what they are
saying, but not a single word is heard on the soundtrack. The extra-
diegetic music of Popol Vuh that accompanies such scenes creates a mood
made all the more eerie by the absence of expected natural sounds.

The minimalist chanting and strumming of Popol Vuh holds the film
together through the repetition of motifs, sometimes associated with the
recurrence of images, such as the slow-motion flight of a bat, which occur
at key moments of the film. But there are musical *contrasts* too, not only
between the modern idiom of Florian Fricke and the earlier music that is
blended into it but also between music and image at different points of

A touch of humour to mitigate the catastrophe

the film. Herzog uses Wagner's 'Rheingold' prelude, with its gradually swelling figurations of the chord of E flat, to convey feelings of awe and apprehension as Jonathan reaches the grandiose mountain top that borders Dracula's realm; but when we hear that music again it accompanies the scurrying of rats whose piping also appears on the soundtrack. The contrast between the original context of the music – the sun rising over the river in which the Rhinemaidens guard their golden hoard – and the plague-bearing rodents is obvious; but the story of greed and ultimate doom that Wagner's prelude heralds has its relevance to the story of Jonathan, who set out to make his fortune only to bring home death and destruction. Irony becomes even more patent at the end when a chorale meant to proclaim the glory of God accompanies Jonathan's ride to become the world's scourge as heir to the 'seed of Belial'. As we have already seen, the appearance of Clemens Scheitz's baffled town official just before this moment introduce a characteristic touch of humour we must not miss in Herzog's films. There is something to laugh at, a moment of the grotesque, in this world from which, as Lucy says, God seems to be infinitely remote, a world in which civic order has irretrievably broken down in face of an all-embracing catastrophe; a world, however, in which, at memorable moments, human beings may assert an existential dignity when confronted by the inevitability of death – a dignity deathless Dracula also seeks to attain.

In the midst of this chequered world Jonathan's journey ultimately leads inwards: into a dark realm of anguish and discontent not unknown to other contributors to the glory of the New German Cinema, though it takes a more overtly political form in Kluge's *Abschied von Gestern* (*Farewell to Yesterday* or *Yesterday Girl,* 1966) and Fassbinder's *Die Ehe der Maria Braun* (*The Marriage of Maria Braun*, 1979) than it does in Herzog's cinematic evocation of a 'Phantom of the Night'. His *Nosferatu* deserves a place, in any history of the cinema, as a milestone on the road travelled by a gifted writer-director who drew on the heritage of Expressionism and Romanticism to take us on a mysterious journey into his, and our, inner world.

Appendix: Herzog's 'Film Narrative'

In the year of *Nosferatu's* premiere, Herzog published a book entitled *Stroszek. Nosferatu. Zwei Filmerzählungen*. The 'cinematic narratives' the title promises conform to Herzog's usual practice of working his plots out in his head and then on paper as a series of scenes with headings briefly indicating location and time of day (for example, 'Stony Path in the Mountains. Dusk', 'Dracula's Castle, Bay Window. Evening'). Dialogues are sketched in and may be modified during the actual filming, with some input by the actors, but Herzog always retained control, keeping his overall scheme firmly in his mind. Within that scheme, however, modifications are possible: some scenes that are found not to work too well in a particular location, or with a particular constellation of actors, may be changed or omitted, their order altered in the cutting room without detriment to the film's structure. The most obvious instance of such a change is the transposition of what was planned as a vision of death just before the end, with graphic shots of mummified corpses in various attitudes, to the very beginning of the film, with programmatic effects already noted.

The two brief extracts I translate below may serve to show, insofar as this is possible in English, how Herzog's desire to link himself to the tradition of German Expressionist film leads to a style that resembles what Henrik Galeen derived and modified from Carl Mayer in his scenario for Murnau's *Nosferatu*.[32]

Stony Path in the Mountains. Dusk. Already dusk is falling; Harker strides vigorously onwards. But what is that? In the last rays of the setting sun his shadow clings to his heels, grows huge and distorted, as though it was not cast by a human being. The shadow takes on a grotesque shape, as if a monster were walking there. Whirring and whistling in the air. From the clouds something emerges – huge! Was that a bat just now drawing a gigantic zigzag onto the sky? Since when are bats that huge? Huge as a pterosaurus? And what is that now? A shadow! Soundlessly the shadow glides over the mountain, grows larger in the valley, disappears, reappears.

Harker stops in his tracks, he sees a whole landscape grow pale. He hastens onwards, his shadow following at his heels. Wolves howl in the distance. There! Were there not eyes in the clouds just now? Something gazing there, in the clouds? Why are the clouds suddenly racing like that? Forty days' worth of clouds in a single hour. Now Jonathan stops after all. The sun has set. The day has crept away like a sick animal.[33]

What this describes are Jonathan's sensations: the film's task is to find landscape and cloudscape images designed to induce in the spectator's mind feelings and sensations akin to Jonathan's – a merging of outer and inner worlds phenomena of nature indicating and symbolising specific human moods while never ceasing to be themselves.

The second extract has the same stylistic traits as the first, but shows in its last sentence a characteristic movement away from the concrete particular to a larger abstraction, from the physical to the metaphysical. Nosferatu becomes not just a bringer of evil, but Evil itself. In the German original what I here translate as 'Evil' (*das Unheil*) is a negation of *das Heil*, a word used in sacred contexts to mean 'salvation'.

Corridor in the Castle. Night. Gaze along the dark corridor. Deadly silence, then, out of the distance, howling of wolves. Nothing stirs, yet something weighs down. There! Did not something move? From the black darkness Nosferatu emerges, he no longer looks human. His face has become rigid, mechanically, unstoppably, he advances. Evil is stalking towards us.[34]

'Da kommt das Unheil gegangen' – it is not just Count Dracula who advances towards Jonathan but Evil itself, an evil that is the very opposite and denial, the negation, of whatever salvation may be hoped for.

Notes

Where omitted in these Notes, full publishing details can be found in the Select Bibliography.

1 Tropp, *Images of Fear*, p. 134.

2 *Dracula*, ed. by Ellmann, pp. xxff.

3 'Capital is dead labour which, vampire-like, lives only by sucking living labour. …' Karl Marx, *Capital* (Harmondsworth: Penguin, 1976), I 342.

4 Ursini and Silver, *The Vampire Film*, pp. 28–9.

5 Don't try this at home! Transfusions are constantly carried out without ascertaining the compatibility of blood types.

6 Tropp, *Images of Fear*, pp. 168–9.

7 *Dracula*, ed. by Ellmann, p. xxiii.

8 Fortunately, a typed copy of Galeen's original screenplay, with Murnau's annotations and alterations, has been preserved and is reprinted in full as an appendix to Lotte Eisner's *Murnau* published in 1979. The original of my quotation appears on p. 393, with Galeen's somewhat strange punctuation. The punctuation is regularised in the English translation of Eisner's book published by Secker and Warburg in the same year. For a facsimile of how this opening title appears in Murnau's film, see Arnold, Farin and Schmid, *Nosferatu. Eine Symphonie des Grauens*, p. 66.

9 My necessarily brief consideration of Stoker's seminal novel may be usefully supplemented by material collected in the Norton Critical Edition of *Dracula*, edited by Nina Auerbach and David J. Skal. This contains interpretative essays by the editors, Stoker's working papers, an opening chapter ('Dracula's Guest'), later omitted, contemporary reviews, a checklist of dramatic and cinematic versions, a wealth of information on such topics as 'suddenly sexual women', 'gender and inversion' and the 'homoerotic' element in the novel, the questionable nobility of a Count who has no servants; and a fuller bibliography than mine. Some recent studies of Murnau's film, which is here considered only in the context of Herzog's play of theme and variations, can be found in the Select Bibliography. The essays assembled in Helmut Prinzler's recent *Murnau. Ein Melancholiker des Films* are particularly useful and authoritative. Comparisons between Herzog's film and Murnau's can be found at key points throughout the present book, particularly in Chapter 4.

10 Quoted in Daniel Lang, *A Backward Look: Germans Remember*, (New York: McGraw-Hill, 1979), pp. 109–10.

11 Cronin, *Herzog on Herzog*, p. 218.

12 Ibid., p. 5.

13 See Herzog's commentary on *Nosferatu* on the DVD listed at the end of the Select Bibliography.

14 Pflaum *et al*., *Werner Herzog*, p. 59.

15 Cronin, *Herzog on Herzog*, p. 2.

16 Ibid., p. viii.

17 'The *Heimatfilm* (homeland film) emerged as the most convenient narrative form for offering a romanticized, …depoliticized, view of country and nation. Quintessential German landscapes like the Bavarian Alps, the Rhine Valley, and the Baltic coast provided idyllic images of rural life where simple peasants lived in harmony with nature' (Hake, *German National Cinema*, p. 76). Hake's valuable account shows how all this could easily connect with fantasies of *Volk* and 'blood and soil' in the Nazi period, and how nostalgic *Heimatfilme* re-emerged in the Federal Republic along with dystopian works.

18 Bock, *Cinegraph*, entry under Schmidt-Reitwein, E 1.

19 Cronin, *Herzog on Herzog*, pp. 108–9.

20 Ibid., pp. 273–5.

21 Effusions printed on the sleeve of a gramophone record (*Kinski spricht Goethe*, amadeo AVRS 2064). Kinski's unreliable autobiography has many references to his sexual exploits that are now unverifiable. Herzog's documentary of his love-hate relationship with his star (*Mein liebster Feind/My Best Fiend*, mediacs AG 14482, DVD) contains an extract from his famous Villon recitations as well as footage of the 'Jesus Tours', and documents his irascible behaviour on set.

22 Elia Kazan, *A Life* (London: Pan Books, 1989), pp. 87–8.

23 Cronin, *Herzog on Herzog*, pp. 80, 256.

24 Christopher Frayling's commentary on the *bfi* DVD listed at the end of the Select Bibliography makes this point along with other valid and interesting observations.

25 N. W. Isenberg, in S. L. Gilman and J. Zipes (eds), *The Yale Companion to Jewish Writing and Thought in German Culture, 1096–1996* (New Haven, CT: Yale University Press, 1997), p. 389, is wrong to call Schreck a 'Jewish actor'. Though never a Nazi, Schreck had no difficulty in bringing the required proof of 'Aryan' descent that ensured that he could continue as a stage actor in Hitler's Germany until his death in 1936. It is worth stressing that his was a tall, handsome presence bearing little resemblance to the horrendously made-up figure that has made him an internationally recognisable icon.

26 Eisner, *Murnau. Mit dem Drehbuch zu Nosferatu*, p. 603. The translation is mine.

27 Review of the Berlin Murnau Restrospective Exhibition, *Frankfurter Allgemeine Zeitung*, 22 February 2003.

28 Biedermeier: a style regarded as characteristic of German art and literature between 1815 and 1848. The word originally expressed an amused contempt for parochial lives and unpolitical attitudes but: 'At the beginning of the twentieth century a consensus grew that this period had, at least in painting, in interior decoration, in furniture, and in architecture, a style which was sober, modest, unpretentious, and yet exhibited a prepossessing elegance' (*The Oxford Companion to German Literature*, ed. by H. and M. Garland, Oxford: Clarendon Press, 1976, pp. 81–2). The literature of the period has also been reinterpreted and revalued by Friedrich Sengle and many others.

29 *Dracula*, ed. by Ellmann, p. 308.

30 Showalter, 'Blood Sell. Vampire Fever and Anxieties for the *Fin de Siècle*', *Times Literary Supplement* (*TLS*), London, 8 January 1993, p. 14.

31 Cronin, *Herzog on Herzog*, pp. 280–1.

32 The comparison can easily be made, thanks to the reprint of Galeen's scenario, with amplifications at the end by Murnau himself, in Eisner's *Murnau*. The Frankfurt edition listed in my bibliography contains the original German text; the London edition has an English translation.

33 Herzog, *Stroszek. Nosferatu*, pp. 96–7.

34 Ibid., p. 110.

Credits

Nosferatu
Phantom der Nacht
Germany/France
1979

Director
Werner Herzog
Producer
Werner Herzog
Screenplay
Werner Herzog
Director of Photography
Jörg Schmidt-Reitwein
Editor
Beate Mainka-Jellinghaus
Art Director
Henning von Gierke
Music
Popol Vuh/Florian Fricke

Production Companies
Michael Gruskoff presents
a Werner Herzog
Filmproduktion
a co-production of
Werner Herzog
Filmproduktion, München,
Gaumont, S.A., Paris
and Zweites Deutsches
Fernsehen
Executive Producer
Walter Saxer
Production Manager
Czechoslovakia:
Rudolf Wolf
Unit Production Manager
Joschi Arpa
[French Unit Production
Manager
Jean-Paul Gibon]

[Dutch Unit Production
Manager
Jaap van Rijs]
Assistant Directors
Remmelt Remmelts
Mirko Tichacek
Script Supervisor
Anja Schmidt-Zäringer
2nd Camera
Michael Gast
Gaffer
Martin Gerbl
Lighting
Anton Urban
[Erich Labermair]
Stills
Dr Claude Chiarini
Special Effects
Cornelius Siegel
Properties
Ulrich Bergfelder
[Propman
Hans Oosterhuis]
Costumes
Gisela Storch
Costume Assistants
Ann Poppel
[Anne Jud, Elisabeth Irmer]
[Wardrobe for Ms Adjani
Claire Fraisse]
Make-up
Reiko Kruk
Dominique Colladant
Hairdressing
Ludovic Paris

Soundtrack
'Das Rheingold' by Richard
Wagner, performed by
Wiener Philharmoniker,
conducted by Sir Georg
Solti (Decca LC 0171);
'Sanctus' from *St. Cecilia*
Mass by Charles Gounod;
'Zinzkaro' by Vokal-
Ensemble Gordela
Sound Supervisor
Harald Maury
Sound Assistant
Jean Fontaine

Cast
Klaus Kinski
Count Dracula
Isabelle Adjani
Lucy Harker
Bruno Ganz
Jonathan Harker
Roland Topor
Renfield
Walter Ladengast
Dr Van Helsing
Dan van Husen
warden
Jan Groth
harbour master
Carsten Bodinus
Schrader, Mina's husband
Martje Grohmann
Mina
Ryk de Gooyer
town official
Clemens Scheitz
town employee
Lo van Hensbergen
inspector

John Leddy
coachman
Margiet van Hartingsveld
maid
Tim Beekman
coffin bearer
Jacques Dufilho
captain of the *Contamana*

[uncredited]
Dr Claude Chiarini
customs inspector
Roger Berry Losch
first mate
Beverly Walker
mother superior
Ulrich Bergfelder
sailor in Delft harbour
Jonathan Cotten
monk
Henning von Gierke
man in square

Anja Schmidt-Zäringer
Walter Saxer
Ann Poppel
Michael Edols
Gisela Storch
Martin Gerbl
diners in the square
Johan te Slaa
bellman
Dominique Colladant
doctor
Werner Herzog
bare-foot man with rats
Rudolf Wolf
Stefan Husar

9,634 feet
107 minutes

Colour by
Eastmancolor

Credits compiled by Markku
Salmi

Select Bibliography and DVD Listing

Arnold, Loy, M. Farin and H. Schmid,
Nosferatu. Eine Symphonie des Grauens
(Munich: Belleville, 2000). (This contains a
facsimile of the colour-toned copy of
Murnau's film prepared by the Münchner
Filmmuseum under the direction of Enno
Patalas.)

Ashbury, Roy, *F. W. Murnau's 'Nosferatu'*
(London: York Press, 2001).

Belford, Barbara, *Bram Stoker. A Biography of
the Author of Dracula* (London:
Weidenfeld and Nicholson, 1996).

Bergfelder, Tim, E. Carter and D. Göktürk
(eds), *The German Cinema Book*
(London: *bfi* Publishing, 2002).

Blumenberg, H. C., *Kinozeit. Aufsätze und
Kritiken zum modernen Film* (Frankfurt am
Main: Fischer, 1980).

Bock, H. M. (ed.), *Cinegraph. Lexikon zum
deutschsprachigen Film* (Munich: edition
text + kritik, 1984ff.).

Cooke, Paul, *German Expressionist Film*
(Harpenden, Herts: Pocket Essentials,
2000).

Corrigan, Thomas (ed.), *The Films of Werner
Herzog. Between Mirage and History*
(London: Methuen, 1986).

———, *New German Film. The Displaced
Image* (Bloomington: Indiana University
Press, rev. edn, 1994).

Cronin, Paul (ed.), *Herzog on Herzog* (London:
Faber & Faber, 2002).

Eisner, Lotte, *Murnau. Mit dem Drehbuch zu
Nosferatu*, ed. by H. Hoffmann and
W. Schober (Frankfurt: Kommunales Kino,
1979).

———, *Murnau*, trans. by G. Mander and
others (London: Secker and Warburg,
1979). This contains the English
translation of Galeen's film script for
Nosferatu. Eine Symphonie des Grauens.

———, *The Haunted Screen. Expressionism
in the German Cinema and the Influence of
Max Reinhardt*, trans. by R. Greaves from
L'Ecran Démoniaque, 1965 (London:
Thames and Hudson, 1973).

Elsaesser, Thomas, *New German Cinema. A
History* (London: Macmillan, 1989).

———, 'Germany, the Weimar Years', in
G. Nowell-Smith (ed.), *The Oxford History
of World Cinema* (Oxford: Oxford
University Press, 1996).

———, *Weimar Cinema and After. Germany's
Historical Imaginary* (London: Routledge,
2000).

Elsaesser, Thomas and M. Wedel, *The BFI
Companion to German Cinema* (London:
bfi Publishing, 1999).

Frayling, Christopher, *Vampyres. Lord Byron to
Count Dracula* (London: Faber & Faber,
1992).

Gandert, Gero (ed.), *1929. Der Film der
Weimarer Republik. Ein Handbuch der
zeitgenössischen Kritik* (Berlin: de Gruyter,
1995).

Gehler, Fred and U. Kasten, *Friedrich Wilhelm
Murnau* (Berlin: Henschel, 1990).

Gregor, Ulrich et al., *Herzog/Kluge/Straub*
(Munich and Vienna: Hanser, 1976).

Hake, Sabine, *German National Cinema*
(London and New York: Routledge, 2000).

Herzog, Werner, *Stroszek. Nosferatu. Zwei
Filerzählungen* (Munich and Vienna:
Hanser, 1979).

———, *Vom Gehen im Eis. München–Paris
23. 11. bis 14. 12. 1974* (Munich and
Vienna: Hanser, 1978).

Jones, Darryl, *Horror. A Thematic History in
Fiction and Film* (London: Arnold, 2002).

Kaes, Anton, 'Film in der Weimarer Republik',
in W. Jacobsen, A. Kaes and
H. H. Prinzler (eds), *Geschichte des*

deutschen Films (Stuttgart and Weimar: Metzler, 1993).

———, 'The New German Cinema', in G. Nowell-Smith (ed.), The Oxford History of World Cinema (Oxford: Oxford University Press, 1996).

———, From Hitler to Heimat. The Return of History as Film (Cambridge, MA: Harvard University Press 1989).

Koebner, Thomas, Idole des deutschen Films. Eine Galerie von Schlüsselfiguren (Munich: edition text&kritik, 1997).

Kracauer, Siegfried, From Caligari to Hitler. A Psychological History of German Film (Princeton, NJ: Princeton University Press, 1947).

Kurtz, Rudolf, Expressionismus und Film (Berlin: Lichtbildbühne, 1926).

Ludlam, Harry, A Biography of Dracula. The Life of Bram Stoker (Slough, Berks: Foulsham, 1962).

McNally, R. T. and R. Florescu, In Search of Dracula. A True History of Dracula and Vampire Legends (New York: Warner, 1973).

Monaco, Paul, Cinema and Society. France and Germany during the Twenties (New York: Elsevier, 1978).

Mulvey, Laura, 'Visual Pleasure and Narrative Cinema', in B. Nichols (ed.), Movies and Methods, Vol. II (Berkeley and London: University of California Press, 1985).

Pflaum, Günther et al., Werner Herzog (Munich and Vienna: Hanser, 1979).

Presser, Beat (ed.), Werner Herzog (Berlin: Jovis Verlag, 2003).

Prinzler, H. H. (ed.), Murnau. Ein Melancholiker des Films (Berlin: Bertz, 2003).

Rentschler, Eric, West German Film-makers on Film (New York and London: Holmes and Meier, 1988).

Salt, Barry, 'From Caligari to Who?', Sight and Sound, vol. 48 no. 2, 1979.

Sandford, John, The New German Cinema (London: Oswald Wolff, 1980).

Stoker, Bram, Dracula, ed. by Maud Ellmann (Oxford: Oxford University Press World Classics, 1998).

———, Dracula, ed. by J. P. Riquelme (Boston and Bedford: Palgrave, 2002).

———, Dracula, ed. by Nina Auerbach and D. J. Skal (New York and London: W. W. Norton & Company, 1997).

Tropp, Martin, Images of Fear. How Horror Stories Helped Shape Modern Culture, 1818–1918 (Jefferson, NC: McFarland, 1999).

Ursini, James and A. Silver, The Vampire Film (London: Tantivy Press, 1975).

DVDs

Nosferatu – a Symphony of Horrors. A Film by F. W. Murnau, Germany 1922. Photoplay Production for Channel Four. Colour-toning and restoration by Enno Patalas and a team at the Munich Film museum. Running time 89 mins. Aspect ratio 1:33:1 (Academy). Music score by James Bernard. Biographies: Commentary by Christopher Frayling. bfi 1997.

[Murnau's] 'Nosferatu', Special Edition two disc DVD. Black and white and colour-toned versions. Running time 90 mins approx. each. Aspect ratio 1:33:1. Music score by Art Zoyd. Commentaries, trailers, artworks and posters. Eureka 2000.

Michael Gruskoff presents a Werner Herzog Film: Nosferatu the Vampyre. Two disc DVD containing German and English versions. Running time 107 mins approx. each. Widescreen. Colour. Commentary by, and interview with, Werner Herzog. Trailers. Anchor Bay Entertainment 2001.

Also Published

Amores Perros
Paul Julian Smith (2003)

L'Argent
Kent Jones (1999)

Blade Runner
Scott Bukatman (1997)

Blue Velvet
Michael Atkinson (1997)

Caravaggio
Leo Bersani & Ulysse Dutoit (1999)

A City of Sadness
Bérénice Reynaud (2002)

Crash
Iain Sinclair (1999)

The Crying Game
Jane Giles (1997)

Dead Man
Jonathan Rosenbaum (2000)

Dilwale Dulhaniya Le Jayenge
Anupama Chopra (2002)

Don't Look Now
Mark Sanderson (1996)

Do the Right Thing
Ed Guerrero (2001)

Easy Rider
Lee Hill (1996)

The Exorcist
Mark Kermode (1997, 2nd edn 1998, rev. 2nd edn 2003)

Eyes Wide Shut
Michel Chion (2002)

Heat
Nick James (2002)

The Idiots
John Rockwell (2003)

Independence Day
Michael Rogin (1998)

Jaws
Antonia Quirke (2002)

L.A. Confidential
Manohla Dargis (2003)

Last Tango in Paris
David Thompson (1998)

Once Upon a Time in America
Adrian Martin (1998)

Pulp Fiction
Dana Polan (2000)

The Right Stuff
Tom Charity (1997)

Saló or The 120 Days of Sodom
Gary Indiana (2000)

Seven
Richard Dyer (1999)

The Shawshank Redemption
Mark Kermode (2003)

The Silence of the Lambs
Yvonne Tasker (2002)

The Terminator
Sean French (1996)

Thelma & Louise
Marita Sturken (2000)

The Thing
Anne Billson (1997)

The 'Three Colours' Trilogy
Geoff Andrew (1998)

Titanic
David M. Lubin (1999)

Trainspotting
Murray Smith (2002)

The Usual Suspects
Ernest Larsen (2002)

The Wings of the Dove
Robin Wood (1999)

Women on the Verge of a Nervous Breakdown
Peter William Evans (1996)

WR – Mysteries of the Organism
Raymond Durgnat (1999)

BFI Modern Classics combine careful research with high-quality writing about contemporary cinema.

If you would like to receive further information about future **BFI Modern Classics** or about other books from BFI Publishing, please fill in your name and address and return this card to us.[*]

(No stamp required if posted in the UK, Channel Islands, or Isle of Man.)

NAME

ADDRESS

POSTCODE

WHICH **BFI MODERN CLASSIC** DID YOU BUY?

[*] In USA and Canada, please return your card to:
University of California Press, 2120 Berkeley Way,
Berkeley, CA 94720 USA

BFI Publishing
21 Stephen Street
FREEPOST 7
LONDON
W1E 4AN